# WE ARE THE LORD'S

WE ARE THE LORD'S
*by* JEAN VIS
Copyright 1955 by
SOCIETY FOR
REFORMED PUBLICATIONS
Grand Rapids, Michigan

PRINTED IN THE UNITED STATES OF AMERICA

# WE ARE THE LORD'S

BY

## JEAN VIS

*Minister of the Word of God in the
Reformed Church in America*

SOCIETY FOR REFORMED PUBLICATIONS
1519 E. Fulton St. — Grand Rapids, Michigan

# CONTENTS

## INTRODUCTION

## THE FIRST PART: OUR SIN

## THE SECOND PART: OUR SALVATION

# THE THIRD PART: OUR SERVICE

# Knowing the Certainty

"That thou mightest know the certainty of those things, wherein thou hast been instructed." Luke 1:4.

*Certainty* is essential in all spheres of knowledge. In his search after truth, the student will learn that this is not easily arrived at. Certainty of the Faith is essential for the Christian who is quite readily swayed by hope and fear. That certainty does not come by way of feeling, vision or mass-enthusiasm, but by instruction of the revealed facts in the Word of God.

*Instruction* in Luke 1:4 is the translation of the word *kat-echo,* whence we have "Catechism." That word Catechism may be outmoded in an age of superficial thinking, but it still has a Biblical foundation and is based on Biblical methods. Jesus was called Teacher. Jesus commanded his disciples to teach all nations. The Christian religion can be taught.

There are principally two methods of teaching these truths, Luther said, just as there are two methods of picking apples. You may shake a tree laden with luscious fruit, or you may pick the apples one by one. So when we open God's Word we are tempted to shake the branches and enjoy the wealth of precious fruit. However, it is eminently proper to handpick and select and study the facts of our faith one by one. Apples keep better by this method. The instruction in the Heidelberg Catechism follows this course.

Objections are sometimes raised against the use of the Heidelberg Catechism in our Reformed Churches. And many outside of the Reformed Church join them in their slogan: "No creed but the Bible." We are told that that method is outdated; we use visual education today. But spiritual things must be spiritually discerned. Some say: "Our people have no desire for doctrinal truths." But mere morals, ethics, politics, book-reviews, etc., will not bring them to Heaven. "We want practical Christianity," some one else remarks. But practical Christianity has as its basis the will of God, which must be known. Some seem to think that the Catechism is a chain to bind them hand and foot; we want to be free! But a blind person accepts the guiding hand of a friend. Is the traveler chained to the correct and visible road signs? Does the sailor fight with his compass? Hosea 4:6 paints the ancient picture of our modern situation: "My people are destroyed for lack of knowledge."

Instruction in the Heidelberg Catechism as a faithful guide brings us that knowledge of the revealed Truth, the whole Truth, the orderly Truth, the experimental Truth.

For the Christian believer that means *certainty,* when he learns to know, believe and love "those things wherein he was instructed."

For the Church it means *unity,* for the 52 Sundays with the 37 Articles and the five Canons are our Forms of Unity in Faith, Form and Fellowship.

1. When was the Heidelberg Catechism composed, and by whom?
2. On what Bible book are its divisions based?
3. Are its contents theoretical or experimental?
4. What does the Constitution of the Reformed Church require regarding its use?
5. Is the Heidelberg Catechism explained in the light of the Bible, or the Bible in the light of the Heidelberg Catechism?
6. What are the Forms of Unity?

For information see *Reformed Standards of Unity,* the Introduction, by Leroy Nixon. Published by the Society for Reformed Publications.

## We Are the Lord's

QUESTION 1 — *What is thy only comfort in life and death?*

ANSWER — That I with body and soul, both in life and death, am not my own, but belong unto my faithful Saviour Jesus Christ, who, with his precious blood, hath fully satisfied for all my sins, and delivered me from all the power of the devil; and so preserves me that without the will of my heavenly Father, not a hair can fall from my head; yea, that all things must be subservient to my salvation; and therefore, by his Holy Spirit, he also assures me of eternal life, and makes me sincerely willing and ready henceforth, to live unto him.

●

Such is the sum and the substance of the 1st Question and Answer of the Heidelberg Catechism. That is the Christian's comfort, his conviction, and his commitment.

Every person has a philosophy of his own, even if he does not know various systems of scholastic philosophy. Every one has a view of life. It is his answer to the question: How do you look at self, the world, life, death? The philosophy of some is Every one for himself. Of others, Get what you can, honestly, or otherwise; A third: Be decent, pay your debts, and no more is needed. So the worldly person: Let us eat, drink, for tomorrow we die. Your philosophy is what you say to yourself in the dark.

That philosophy is your yard-stick; it is the colored glass through which you view life. But many glasses are distorted, dirty. Thus wrong conclusions are made; troubles arise; mistakes result; life is wasted.

The Christian has a philosophy too. How do you look upon life, what is your interpretation, what is your comfort? is asked. And the Instructor points to the revealed Word of God. Come what may, in life and death, for time and eternity: *We are the Lord's!* Rom. 14:8.

In the very first statement we are face to face with the fundamentals of our Christian faith. Here we stand! The healing fountain of the blood of Christ is full and free. The devil is overthrown. Here we are in the Father's preservation and providence.

So it is stated, that the anxious inquirer will be attracted and continue to follow instructions to obtain that comfort. So it expresses the joy of the believer, as he traces the way of God with men, in all what is to follow.

Theo-centric and Trinitarian is this full gamut of our Christian faith. God the Son saves and delivers; God the Father preserves and protects; God the Spirit assures us of eternal life, and makes us willing to live unto Him.

That is a Christian's comfort. That is his *only* comfort. That must be our commitment. That furnishes us with the explanation of life's trials; that gives us strength for the task ahead. That is our Christian view which opens worldwide vistas of salvation and joy when we can face all issues and be a blessing to all mankind, when we can truly say: *We are the Lord's!*

1. Does this Lord's Day require a detailed study in its answer?
2. What does "comfort" mean?
3. What does "only" imply?
4. What two activities are ascribed to Jesus?
5. What two activities are ascribed to God the Father?
6. What two activities are ascribed to God the Holy Spirit?
7. What practical implications follow when "we are the Lord's"?

# Three Signposts

QUESTION 2 — *How many things are necessary for thee to know, that thou, enjoying this comfort, mayest live and die happily?*

ANSWER — Three; the first, how great my sins and miseries are; the second, how I may be delivered from all my sins and miseries; the third, how I shall express my gratitude to God for such deliverance.

●

How shall we arrive at that state of spiritual happiness whereby we know that we are the Lord's? How many things must we know? Three signposts are pointed out to us on the way to Heaven: *Sin, Saviour, Service.*

That outline of the Catechism is based on the Epistle to the Romans. All Christian people do not begin there. A Bible was handed to a Mohammedan scholar, Dr. S. Zwemer tells us, on her request to learn about the Christian religion. She read Genesis and liked it. She read Exodus and found it interesting. She proceeded to Leviticus and Deuteronomy and became perplexed, for to her it was as dry as a desert. Disappointed, she returned the Bible.

The Heidelberg Catechism does not lead you that way on good authority. Jesus began his earthly ministry by saying, Repent and believe. Jesus ended his earthly ministry by commanding that repentance and remission of sins should be preached in his name. John the Baptist, Paul and Philip pursued that course.

We must know our personal *Sin,* not measured by man's standards, but by God's requirements. Nor is a complete knowledge expected, for God's commandments are preached (Qu. 115) "that all our lifetime we may learn more and more our sinful nature." But we need a conviction of sin, which comes when we see ourselves in the mirror of the revealed will of God, applied by the Holy Spirit.

We must know our *Saviour.* Merely to know his sin did not save Judas. Jesus said to the Pharisees (John 9:41): "If ye were blind, ye would have no sin. But now ye say: We see; therefore your sin remaineth."

We must know a life of *Service:* gratitude, as an inevitable result and visible evidence. All Biblical teaching, preaching, prayer, and praise contain elements of one or two or all three of these items.

This threefold knowledge is different from scientific knowledge. Personal reaction is immaterial in the pursuit of science. But not so in religion. Here knowledge is subjective, personal, experimental in its appropriation.

Even at this early position in the Heidelberg Catechism we part company with those whose appeal to the unconverted is in substance: "Jesus loves you and died for you. You ought to accept him as your Saviour." Without condemning their efforts, we believe that to obtain Biblical results, we should follow Biblical instructions. On the way to Heaven we wish to travel on the King's Highway. And on the King's Highway there are three signposts: *Sin, Saviour, and Service.*

1. Name the three essential truths we should know.
2. Should we know them mentally or experimentally?
3. How are we convinced of sin?
4. Do we know the full extent of sin?
5. Does need of repentance and remission of sin indicate our need?
6. By whose standards are our sins measured?
7. Whence is our knowledge of our Saviour?
8. What does a life of gratitude include?

# THE FIRST PART
## *Our Sin*

### The Mystery of Our Misery

QUESTION 3 — *Whence knowest thou thy misery?*

ANSWER — Out of the law of God.

QUESTION 4 — *What doth the law of God require of us?*

ANSWER — Christ teaches us that briefly, Matt. xxii:37-40, "Thou shalt love the Lord thy God with all thy heart, and with all thy soul, and with all thy mind, and with all thy strength. This is the first and great command; and the second is like to this, Thou shalt love thy neighbor as thyself. On these two commands hang the whole law and the prophets."

QUESTION 5 — *Canst thou keep all these things perfectly?*

ANSWER — In no wise; for I am prone by nature to hate God and my neighbor.

●

The *Mystery* of our misery is our ignorance of our misery. Reasonably, we would expect that we knew all about that. If we are tortured by physical distress, we can tell! No, not always. Hidden disease can be detected by the skilled physician when the patient is unaware of his trouble. So the X-rays of God's law reveal the hidden cancer of human misery and sin, so that the remedy may be desired and applied.

Misery is not sin. Misery is the result of sin. Misery is the word for "outlandish" (ellendig) which means to be without home and its protection.

The natural man does not know that he is far from the Father's home. Many of the captives felt perfectly at home in Babylon. Paul did not know about coveting being sin. Jesus told the Laodiceans, "Thou knowest not that thou art wretched and miserable" (Rev. 3:17).

Sin (Latin *sine*) also means "without." We are without God's image. Hence our misery is five-fold: we are "without" True Knowledge, Righteousness, Holiness, our Home and Happiness.

And we do not know that. We are not like Abraham, who knew he was a pilgrim; we have no memory of the Father's house, like the Prodigal son. We might have known by our inability to cure diseases; to ward off death; to maintain peace. Our asylums and hospitals and battlefields could inform us. When troubles become too evident, we try to cure without knowing the cause. We are in a frenzy. In our helplessness we sink deeper and deeper into the quicksand of despair by our man-made efforts.

The *Measure* of our Misery is indicated by God's commandments. Voluminous like a lawyer's library? Complicated like our Federal statutes? No, just two: Love God and love thy neighbor.

Loving God means to acknowledge, obey and serve God with all our heart, soul, mind and strength. To love our neighbor means to seek his welfare and not his hurt. This summary is not voluminous, nor complicated, but comprehensive, for "on these two commandments hang all the law and the prophets."

Now the *Misunderstanding* of our Misery must still be added. We do not readily agree that we are "prone to hate God and our neighbor." We imagine ourselves respectable citizens; we are law-abiding, friendly people! The Rich Young Ruler expressed himself in this way. We do not understand that "prone by nature" indicates our darkness, debt, defilement, disease, death, for such is sin.

Then we understand Paul's experience: "Wretched man that I am!" The one ray of hope is when we like Paul learn to trust our Saviour, so that with Paul we too can say: "I thank God through Jesus Christ our Lord."

Guthrie wrote: "Man's misery, not his merit, is the magnet that draws the Saviour from the skies."

1. Mention laws of God in creation.
2. What laws did God establish for our moral and spiritual welfare?
3. How do you distinguish laws of God and those ascribed to fate?
4. When quoting the law, why is Matt. 22 mentioned here in the catechism and not Exodus 20?
5. Is the law merely a mirror to see our possible perfection? Rom. 3:20.
6. Does loving our neighbor lead us to loving God?
7. What does "prone by nature" indicate in regard to the source of that love?
8. Why do Christians need to be reminded of the law of God? Titus 3:3
9. Why is the law read and preached in the worship of the congregation?

## Sin Entered

QUESTION 6 — *Did God then create man so wicked and perverse?*

ANSWER — By no means; but God created man good, and after his own image, in righteousness and true holiness, that he might rightly know God his Creator, heartily love him and live with him in eternal happiness to glorify and praise him.

QUESTION 7 — *Whence then proceeds this depravity of human nature?*

ANSWER — From the fall and disobedience of our first parents, Adam and Eve, in Paradise; hence our nature is become so corrupt, that we are all conceived and born in sin.

●

An important problem in religion and philosophy is *How* sin entered into the world. That is important, for on the explanation of the cause depends the suggestion for the cure. Whence is evil?

*Not By Creation.* God saw that everything was good. (Gen. 1:27, 31).

God created man in his own image, that is, in true knowledge, righteousness and holiness, so that man had a perfect *Personality,* revealed in his reason, will and judgment; *Spirituality* in holiness of worship and work, not merely acquired, but as his personal possession — not neutral, not evenly balanced, **but positively** good; and *Immortality* to glorify and praise God in eternal happiness. Article 14 of our Belgic Confession states: "Man's will in all respects co-inciding with the will of God." And the Third Canon of Dort: "Man was adorned with true and saving knowledge of God."

However, Socinians held that God created evil as well as good, a sort of Dualism affiliated with this false position as if there were a god for good and a god for evil. Socialists find the source of evil in society. Evolution sees evil in the process of becoming good in the eons to come. To these and many other human explanations, the Bible says, No, not by creation, but by:

*Separation*: the fall and disobedience of our first parents. The fall as described in Genesis 3 was man's fall from that high estate. This was by no means a fall upward, as some modernists have dared to proclaim; the fall is a fall downward. Man fell from that high position by disobeying God and listening to the devil. No need of any argument as to how great or how small that disobedience was. The flower that is separated from its stem cannot be restored. The tree that falls by the lightning's flash or by the wood-cutter's axe is down.

There is more than this. As Adam was the head of the Covenant the fall affected posterity. Consequently we read in Gen. 1:27, "God created man in his own image," and then we read concerning Adam in Gen. 5:3, "He begat a son in his likeness." When the fountain is unclean, the water is impure. Sickness, death, thorns in the soul and in the soil resulted. No "tabula rasa" is the human soul. Evil is in us, not by imitation as the Pelagians held, but by implanation. "Our nature is so corrupt that we are all conceived and born in sin" (Ps. 51). So Art. III, 3 of the Canons of Dort: "We are all born as children of wrath." Original sin is the trail of the serpent.

So the curse comes to us in line with man's disobedience: the obedience of Jesus to the will of God, in reply to the fall, the *Incarnation* of God in Christ, the first step in the Humiliation, when Heaven stooped to lift us up, is the hope of our restoration.

1. To what three holy offices was man created?
2. What is the image of God in man?
3. What does the N. T. teach us concerning the historical truth of Genesis 3? Rom. 5:12.
4. Which two words in the Catechism describe Adam's fall?
5. How does original sin and pollution affect Adam's descendants?
6. Who teach that man's free will enables him to turn to God?
7. What is the promise and the penalty of the Covenant of works? Romans 5:12-21.

## At the Cross Roads

QUESTION 8 — *Are we then so corrupt, that we are wholly incapable of doing any good, and inclined to all wickedness?*

ANSWER — Indeed we are, except we are regenerated by the Spirit of God.

QUESTION 9 — *Doth not God then do injustice to man, by requiring from him in his law, that which he cannot perform?*

ANSWER — Not at all: for God made man capable of performing it; but man, by the instigation of the devil, and his own wilful disobedience, deprived himself and all his posterity of those divine gifts.

●

Here we stand at the cross-roads of Protestant affirmation. It pertains to mighty subjects like total depravity, free will, innate goodness, and spiritual attainments. Can we or can we not do anything spiritually good?

Many Christian people who shared the road with us part company with us on this issue. This has become the Great Divide among Protestants. For generations Arminians and Calvinists have debated which direction to follow. What still is the rock of offense for those with leanings toward human will and choice in things spiritual, which needs only a certain enlightenment to come to full fruition, has become the cornerstone in Calvinism of God's free sovereignty and man's total depravity.

Calvinism maintains that "in us, that is in our flesh, dwelleth no good thing." Calvinists believe Jesus' statement in John 15:5. They included in their Confession John 1:5 (Art. 14): "The light shineth in darkness, and the darkness comprehended it not." And they wrote in Canon III: "They neither will nor can return to God, nor improve their corrupt nature, without the grace of the Holy Spirit unto regeneration."

Yet Reformed people need to know that both the Confession (14) and the Canon (III, 4) mention "small sparks left in us" and "some light of nature." How do we reconcile that? In the fact that man's fall still left him with a human nature, he became neither devil nor brute beast. He lost his sinless nature, but not his essence. We are not sticks and stones. But these "sparks" never burst into flames of holiness. Man cannot arrive at saving knowledge by his own efforts. The Bible maintains this; history proves this; heathenism illustrates this. Modernism denies it, but cannot give proof of its negation. Human nature is too proud to accept this. But the child of God learns it in the school of Christ. John 6:44 — "No one can come unto me, except the Father which hath sent me draw him."

Are we then incapable of doing any good? We can render civil and moral good; we can feed the hungry and engage in philanthropy; many make much of "common grace" and "practical Christianity," yes, they manifest some good toward their fellowmen and we appreciate that. They are like a clock without main spring that shows time accurately twice a day, and does some good. But it is dead. And they that are in the flesh cannot please God. We must be regenerated by the Holy Spirit.

Have we no free will then? Yes, but a sinful free will: a will to do evil. When a man seeks God, it is God who worketh in us both to will and to do.

"Except" contains a humiliating and yet comforting truth. Yes, there is a way to God, but that is not the way of man's moral nature; not the road of law-obedience, but the way of the Holy Spirit and the Gospel of Christ. That way we will follow.

1. What is the great division at this point?
2. Is self-improvement sufficient?
3. Is education or reformation sufficient?
4. Have we by nature the will to be saved?
5. Can our moral nature attain to salvation?
6. What good can the natural man do?
7. Discuss man's free will.
8. Why is regeneration necessary?

## Against the Most High Majesty of God

QUESTION 10 — *Will God suffer such disobedience and rebellion to go unpunished?*

ANSWER — By no means: but is terribly displeased with our original as well as actual sins; and will punish them in his just judgment, temporally and eternally, as he hath declared, "Cursed is every one that continueth not in all things, which are written in the book of the law to do them."

QUESTION 11 — *Is not God then also merciful?*

ANSWER — God is indeed merciful, but also just; therefore his justice requires that sin which is committed against the most high majesty of God, be also punished with extreme that is, with everlasting punishment both of body and soul.

●

Lines about eternal punishment should be written wet with tears of our soul. Words thus spoken must have the hush of awe.

The root of bitterness, of ridicule and doubt concerning this subject finds fertile soil in our ignorance concerning the person sinned against, and our misconception of the antithesis between God's holiness and man's sinfulness. All sin is committed against God. And God is not described here as "our kind heavenly Father," but as the "most high majesty of God." Our Canon 2, 1 speaks of the "Infinite Majesty." When we have that Biblical conception of God and his holiness, sin is not merely perverted indulgence of our natural appetite: it is *lese majeste*: sin against the Infinite Majesty leads to infinite destiny.

Three questions are asked concerning this punishment:

*Is It Just?*

We cannot obey the law, and still God demands it! Adam evaded it: "The woman thou gavest me." "I knew thou art a man reaping where thou didst not sow." Excuses everywhere, always. However, God made man capable of performing the law, but man by the instigation of the devil and his own willful disobedience, deprived himself and all his posterity of those divine gifts. Art. 16: "God is just in leaving others in their fall and misery, in which they have cast themselves."

*Is It Certain?*

Perhaps sin will go unpunished, as happens everywhere around us! Not every criminal faces the judge. No thunderbolt strikes us, when we transgress the Ten Commandments. Original sin I disclaim and with actual sin I can afford to take a chance, so speaks a rebellious voice in the troubled silence of the hall of justice of man's accusing conscience. But the law of retribution is deeply carved in our universe. Laws of health require obedience or trouble comes. Parents, courts and governments have laws and execute them. In good literature we look for "poetic justice." This world would be chaos if there were no ultimate justice. It may take time, for these mills grind slowly, but no one escapes. Galatians 3:10. Canon 2 : ". . . which punishment we cannot escape, unless God's righteousness is satisfied."

*Is It Fearful?*

Hebrews 10:31. What Jesus said about the place "where the worm dieth not and the fire is not quenched" may be figurative but is not fiction. Jesus' pronouncements concerning the place of torment in parable and preaching are more positive and numerous than those of all sacred writers combined. Who dares to accept Jesus' kind invitation to everlasting life, and not heed his solemn warning against everlasting punishment? Our Protestant pulpits have soft-pedaled this doctrine by substituting for hell-fire, psychological essays on "Peace of Mind" with a hypnotism of evasion. No wonder Satan makes inroads in Church and Society.

The proof of and the hope in that fearfulness is evident when Jesus bore our punishment: the chastisement of our sin was upon him! Him who knew no sin, God made sin on our behalf. Would you see the fearfulness of the curse of sin? Go to dark Gethsemane and linger at cross-crowned Calvary. There is the demonstration and the divine miracle of substitution. And we cast our anchor there.

1. What is original sin?
2. Name three spheres in which actual sin is committed.
3. What attributes of God demand punishment for sin?
4. How is sin punished temporally? eternally?
5. Does God's mercy excuse man's sin?
6. What are sins of omission and commission?
7. Does the Bible teach everlasting punishment or annihilation?

# THE SECOND PART
# *Our Salvation*

## The Way of Escape

QUESTION 12 — *Since then by the righteous judgment of God, we deserve temporal and eternal punishment, is there no way by which we may escape that punishment, and be again received into favor?*

ANSWER — God will have his justice satisfied; and therefore we must make this full satisfaction, either by ourselves or by another.

QUESTION 13 — *Can we ourselves then make this satisfaction?*

ANSWER — By no means: but on the contrary we daily increase our debt.

QUESTION 14 — *Can there be found anywhere, one who is a mere creature, able to satisfy for us?*

ANSWER — None; for first, God will not punish any other creature for the sin which man hath committed; and further, no mere creature can sustain the burden of God's eternal wrath against sin, so as to deliver others from it.

QUESTION 15 — *What sort of a mediator and deliverer then must we seek for?*

ANSWER — For one who is very man, and perfectly righteous; and yet more powerful than all creatures; that is, one who is also very God.

The scapegoat and other Old Testament ceremonial laws teach us the seriousness of sin and its consequences and God's revealed way of escape: by way of substitution or satisfaction. These ceremonies are fulfilled in Christ, our Mediator, concerning whom the prophets spoke; whom John the Baptist pointed out as the Lamb of God; who himself said: I am the way. Concerning our Mediator we learn in this Lord's Day:—

*The Necessity* of this Mediator. Three other "ways" are overruled. First, that perhaps God will not punish sin, hence no need of mediation. The answer comes—without hesitation: God will have his justice satisfied. Then it might be possible that we ourselves could make that satisfaction! But we increase our debt daily. We have a debt of 10,000 talents and we do not have one penny to pay. That way, then, is closed too. And the third way is a dead end, too: can we find a creature to pay for us? That bears looking into, but the negative answer is based on the fact that sin as debt is not merely a financial obligation, but has moral and spiritual relation, so that God will not punish any other creature for the sin we have committed. That excludes other "creatures" — those who are created, like saints, angels, priests or popes and their efforts or claims in Church or Sacraments. The Bible speaks of *one* name under Heaven. Hence it is stated in Article 26 of our Confession: We believe that we have no access to God, except through our Mediator, Jesus Christ.

*The Personality* of this Mediator. What sort of a person must he be? One who is very man and perfectly righteous, and yet more powerful than all creatures, that is, One who is also very God. Inasmuch as the personality of the Mediator is discussed in the next Lord's Day we do not here enlarge upon the dual nature of Christ. Suffice it to say that our Mediator must be both God and man. God . . . to bear the infinite curse and to bring God to man. He must be man to have a feeling for our infirmities and to bring man to God. Jesus Christ is perfect man in His wonderful birth; sinless life; humility; compassion; obedience to the Law; and willing to die under the law, not for self but for others. Jesus Christ is also very God with power to save; with ability to bear the wrath of God; with strength to overcome the devil and our last enemy, death; to be our High Priest in Heaven, who will receive all glory when the Kingdoms of this world become the Kingdom of our Christ.

*The Activity* of this Mediator. Thus Moses stood between Israel and God; thus Judah in his intercessory prayer became a "surety" for the lad; thus Job looked for a "days-man betwixt us." So we hail with joy our Mediator! Yes, there is a way of escape through our Mediator, Jesus Christ: the only One revealed, the only One who is able; the only One who is sufficient!

1. What is the relation between God's love and God's demand for full satisfaction for sin?
2. Does not God's forgiveness permit the sinner to escape?
3. Why can the sinner not pay for his sin?
4. Why can no mere creature — angel or saint — pay for sin?
5. What are the requirements for a true Mediator?
6. Is the source of divine grace in Christ or in the Trinity?
7. What is the substitutionary sacrifice of Christ?
8. What is the Covenant of Grace? Gen. 3:15, Gen. 17:7.

# Two Divine Musts

QUESTION 16 — *Why must he be very man and also perfectly righteous?*

ANSWER — Because the justice of God requires that the same human nature which has sinned should likewise make satisfaction for sin; and one, who is himself a sinner, cannot satisfy for others.

QUESTION 17 — *Why must he in one person be also very God?*

ANSWER — That he might by the power of his Godhead, sustain in his human nature, the burden of God's wrath; and might obtain for, and restore to us, righteousness and life.

●

Having considered what manner of mediator we must seek, we now stand face to face with the question what manner of mediator God requires. Let no one minimize this issue. We admit that this is readily ignored, for even in man's redemption he is still so human that he thinks first and foremost, and almost exclusively, of man and his needs. So when we celebrate the coming of the Mediator at Christmas we emphasize the Mother and the manger, the cradle and the Christ-child. It is so attractive and so human, the little Lord Jesus asleep in the hay. And to some of us who think a bit more deeply come streams of hope and joy and peace, and in the glow of Christmas candles the love for our own children shines more brightly, and justly so. But when we confess that the very center of our faith is not our salvation, but God's glory, does it ever occur to us to ask why the Incarnation was necessary from God's side? *Cur Deus Homo?* Why *must* our Mediator be a true and sinless man? Why *must* he be at the same time true God? Here the Gospel trumpet gives no uncertain sound, when two reasons are mentioned for these divine requirements.

(I) *God's Unchanging Justice.* Man, and man in his representative state, humanity, sinned against God. Punishment was pronounced upon him and all humanity, for God's justice cannot let sin go unpunished. And God's justice also required that this punishment be visited upon the same human nature which sinned. Not an angel or a newly created being could take humanity's place. But man himself cannot satisfy the divine demand, hence God's justice requires that our Mediator must be a true and sinless man. But why pin-point God's righteousness in this case, when we speak of the Gospel of Love? Because the Gospel is the Gospel of righteousness: Rom. 1:16. In the Gospel the righteousness of God is revealed from faith to faith. And in man's sin, the question underlying the Gospel of Love is: who will be victorious? Will it be God's justice demanding punishment or man's sin in setting up his own standard of right and wrong? For God to be just and the justifier of the unjust, this divine *must* is satisfied in Christ. In him "mercy and truth are met together; righteousness and peace have kissed each other" (Ps. 85:10).

(II) *God's Infinite Merit.* When we speak of our Mediator as a true and sinless man, we still ask: Can he bear the burden of God's wrath? Can he pay humanity's debt? How great, how powerful must our Mediator be, so that he could be Mediator for all time for all men? What did God require? That in the power of his Godhead he might, in his manhood, bear the burden of God's wrath. That means that God's wrath is so great that no one can measure it or satisfy it; it is infinite. Only God is infinite, and no matter how great the weight of sin, God's infinite merit is greater. Thus by the power of his Godhead Christ bore the burden of God's wrath. Calvary was no token payment. The Cross is no mere emblem. Our Lord's cry, "It is finished," was no meaningless expression.

Now that the slate is clean, the pardoned sinner still needs positive assets. And again only by the power of his Godhead can our Mediator restore unto us righteousness and life; no one else could give that to us. Such a Mediator is required by God's justice and infinite merit, and such a Mediator God provides in our Lord Jesus Christ.

When the Advent season rolls around we rejoice again in the marvel of the Incarnation, the evidence of God's love. But now we know that Bethlehem's miracle was not only an evidence of God's love or a stimulus for our love for childhood. For against the background of Revelation stand out in bold relief the divine requirements of our Mediator: God's unchanging justice and God's infinite merit. Thus we confirm our faith, "But of him are ye in Christ Jesus, who of God is made unto us wisdom and righteousness and sanctification and redemption" (I Cor. 1:30).

1. What do we consider God's requirements for our Mediator?
2. Why did God's righteousness require our Mediator to have a human nature?

3. What did Christ's human nature consist of?
4. Why did God's infinite merit require our Mediator to have a divine nature?
5. What is the relation between the human and divine nature of Christ?
6. If Jesus did not suffer in his divine nature, what did his divine nature contribute?
7. What are the positive blessings our Mediator gives us?
8. Why is Christ's death sufficient for all men?
9. Why is Christ's death not efficient for all men?


## In One Person

QUESTION 18 — *Who then is that Mediator who is in one person both very God and a real, righteous man?*

ANSWER — Our Lord Jesus Christ "who of God is made unto us wisdom and righteousness, and sanctification, and redemption."

QUESTION 19 — *Whence knowest thou this?*

ANSWER — From the Holy Gospel, which God himself revealed first in Paradise; and afterwards published by the patriarchs and prophets; and was pleased to represent it, by the shadows of sacrifices and the other ceremonies of the law; and lastly has accomplished it by his only-begotten Son.

●

Gladly would we know more about this Mediator! "In one Person," merits the emphasis in the doctrine of the Mediator. So often we speak of the two natures, the three offices of Christ, but even at Christmas we do not sufficiently magnify our faith "in one Person." That has been the rock of offense of many heresies, but this blessed mystery of the Incarnation has become the believer's sheet anchor for wisdom, righteousness, sanctification and redemption. Belgic Confession 18 and 19.

Whence do we know this? And the 19th question and answer speaks of four distinctive streams of divine Revelation confluent in our Mediator: the Gospel in Paradise; the Patriarchs and Prophets; the ceremonial law; and God's only begotten Son. Our knowledge of the Mediator comes from the whole Bible, as Jesus himself exemplifies in Luke 24:27, 44.

From the study of the complete Revelation we learn that our Mediator is in one Person: 1. *Very God.* The conception by the

Holy Spirit, the Virgin Birth are held before our wondering gaze! Divine names, honors, powers, attributes are given to Jesus. He is very God to a. support his human nature in bearing the wrath of God; b. to supply infinite worth to his sacrifice; c. to subdue our enemies, Satan and Death; d. to assure us of eternal life.

*2. Real Man.* Article 16 states: "That is with body and soul, not in appearance but in reality." Not in changing his divine nature into human, for the Godhead is immutable; not by mixing the two natures, but by adopting humanity in the unity of his person. His humanity is not changed into deity, hence is not omnipresent like Lutherans teach; it is not produced by magic like the Roman Catholic priest pretends; he did not take it from Heaven, but as Article 18 states: "His humanity is from the loins of David, the womb of Mary, the tribe of Judah, the seed of Abraham, and is become like unto his brethren, sin excepted."

*3. Righteous Man.* Both friend and foe testified to that. A righteous person is needed to bear the sin committed in the flesh. As a righteous person, Jesus suffered in his human nature, and not in his divine nature as some of our hymns maintain.

*4. God and Man.* In the unity of His person His work as man is the work of the Son of God, and as such has infinite merit and is sufficient for all.

Now that merit unfolds itself into a four-fold blessing for the believer: wisdom, righteousness, sanctification and redemption. Such a wonderful Mediator is our Lord Jesus Christ "in one person"!

1. Why must the Mediator have a human nature?
2. How is this brought about in Christ's Incarnation?
3. What twofold reason is taught as to why Christ must be divine?
4. Prove Christ's divine nature.
5. What is the meaning of the names Jesus and Christ?
6. What is the relation between the two natures of Christ?
7. How did our Lord Jesus Christ merit our salvation?
8. Where in the Bible is Christ as Mediator revealed, published, represented and accomplished?

# Credo . . . I Believe

QUESTION 20 — *Are all men then, as they perished in Adam, saved by Christ?*

ANSWER — No; only those who are ingrafted into him and receive all his benefits, by a true faith.

QUESTION 21 — *What is true faith?*

ANSWER — True faith is not only a certain knowledge, whereby I hold for truth all that God has revealed to us in his word, but also an assured confidence, which the Holy Ghost works by the Gospel, in my heart; that not only to others but to me also, remission of sin, everlasting righteousness and salvation are freely given by God, merely of grace, only for the sake of Christ's merits.

●

Here we feel the very heart beat of the Catechism: credo — the keynote of the Christian's life! To steer this course, no Universalist in salvation needs to apply to take the helm and the anxious Inquirer is given his sailing orders: the *necessity* and the *essence* of true faith. Throughout the rest of the journey the Catechism follows these orders in dealing successively with the Contents, the Results, the Growth and the Fruit of true faith.

The *Necessity* of true faith. By faith we are ingrafted into Christ, and become one with him, and in this union we receive all his benefits. Romans 3:28. Christ's life flows through the ingrafted branches. Believing in him we have everlasting life. John 3:16. Without him, we do not see life. John 3:36. Our Confession in Article 22 states: "He who possesses Jesus Christ through faith, has his complete salvation in him."

The *Essence* of true faith. It is distinguished from historic faith. Such a faith holds that sacred history is true, that Christ was a historic person, but it does not change the heart. The devil is said to have a similar faith, Jas. 2:1.

It is also distinguished from miraculous faith: the faith to believe the miracles of the Bible; or faith to be healed but not to be saved, with present day reference to Faith Healing. Paul mentions a faith that could remove mountains, yet fell short. I Cor. 13:3.

It also differs from temporary faith, which in some respects is most like true faith. This is aroused in mass enthusiasm or born from compassion or fear. Jesus speaks in the Parable of the Sower of temporary faith.

Two elements are described in Question 21 as the essentials of true faith:

1. *A Certain Knowledge* whereby I hold for truth all that God has revealed to us in his Word. "Certain" here means "definite" and not "uncertain" as sometimes our language permits. "Definite" Bible knowledge in teaching and preaching always was the pride and joy of the Reformed Church!

2. *An Assured Confidence* which the Holy Ghost works by the Gospel in my heart. Faith is a matter of the heart, not the head only. It is knowledge, but knowledge that transforms life. Now the four fundamental facts of that assured confidence are here taught. They form an excellent test for confession of faith for prospective Church members and they present a profitable guide for the reality of faith in our heart. We have an assured confidence that God has freely given us: a) Remission of sin; that comes first for the name "Jesus" means just that. b) Everlasting righteousness imputed unto us through Christ, in contrast with both personal and legal righteousness, which are not everlasting. c) Salvation by grace, not even our faith being the meriting cause. d) Only for the sake of Christ's merits. Examine yourself whether you are in the faith, for that is a matter of life or death!

1. What do Universalists teach in regard to salvation?
2. Is grace inherited, like sin is inherited?
3. Does the saved person stand alone, or is he ingrafted into Christ?
4. Who does the ingrafting: fate, human will, or God?
5. What is the place of grace and faith in our salvation?
6. What are minimum requirements of knowledge and confidence as elements of true faith?
7. By what means does the Holy Spirit work faith in our hearts?
8. Why are the Twelve Articles of our Faith called the Apostles' Creed?

# Our Christian Faith

QUESTION 22 — *What is then necessary for a Christian to believe?*

ANSWER — All things promised us in the Gospel, which the articles of our Catholic undoubted Christian faith briefly teach us.

QUESTION 23 — *What are these articles?*

ANSWER — I. I believe in God, the Father Almighty, maker of heaven and earth:

II. And in Jesus Christ, his only begotten Son, our Lord:

III. Who was conceived by the Holy Ghost, born of the Virgin Mary:

IV. Suffered under Pontius Pilate; was crucified, dead and buried: He descended into hell:

V. The third day he rose again from the dead.

VI. He ascended into heaven, and sitteth at the right hand of God the Father Almighty:

VII. From thence he shall come to judge the quick and the dead.

VIII. I believe in the Holy Ghost:

IX. I believe in a Holy Catholic Church; the communion of saints:

X. The forgiveness of sins:

XI. The resurrection of the body.

XII. And the life everlasting. Amen.

QUESTION 24 — *How are these articles divided?*

ANSWER — Into three parts; the first is of God the Father, and our creation; the second of God the Son, and our redemption; the third of God the Holy Ghost, and our sanctification.

●

True or saving faith having been described, our attention here is directed to the contents of that faith. The Apostles' Creed, or the 2 articles, divided in three parts concerning God the Father and creation, concerning God the Son and salvation, and concerning the Holy Spirit and Sanctification are here placed before us as the promises of the Gospel which we as Christians must believe.

To those who object to the sharp outlines of its contents, we reply that spiritual ignorance is no bliss. "Do you believe in Jesus" may be the only test for many, but still the question remains: "What think ye of Christ? Whose Son is he?" To repent and believe the Gospel is a good Biblical basis for discipleship, but then again we ask what is meant by the Gospel when many have an idea of the good tidings of the goodness of God and forget his righteousness.

It is true, we live in the Gospel dispensation, but even in the Old Testament the Gospel was preached to those in prison, and we speak of the Gospel in Ezekiel and other prophets. Strictly speaking God's Word contains both Law and Gospel. The Law is what God demands and the Gospel is what God promised. But there was Gospel for those under the Law, and there is Law for those under the Gospel. That Gospel came to our first parents (Gen. 3:15), and it is incarnated in Christ.

Even to enumerate all the promises of God would require extensive Scriptural knowledge. But some are so essential that surely a minimum is requisite. How thankful we are for that summary in the Apostles' Creed, which is so old that its age cannot be determined and which is so up-to-date that its form needs no revision!

The Apostles' Creed! What a wonderful statement of our Christian faith. The twelve articles were not submitted by the apostles, one each, as some say. It is the Apostles' Creed because that was what the Apostles, eyewitnesses of Christ, believed and preached.

Now when we say: "I believe," and then confess our faith as here expressed, we make a personal, experimental confession of our universal, undoubted, Christian faith. Just as we learned to say, and after that to pray the Lord's Prayer, so we learned to repeat the Creed. And having found through God's Holy Spirit the application of these words in our hearts, we then learned to confess the Creed, and our soul was refreshed when in detailed description we confessed the work of God from Creation to Salvation and to Sanctification, of which we through God's grace form a blessed part.

How wonderful is this basis for our faith: What must a Christian believe? It is not what must a Presbyterian believe, or a Methodist, or one of the Reformed persuasion. . . but, embracing them all, a Christian. Let no one rob us of this heritage, by saying,

"No Creed but the Bible." Those who thus speak ofttimes substitute their own narrow interpretation as a creed which they insist on far more strictly and strongly and which is not entitled to the praise: "Universal and undoubted."

How rich is this treasure for the believer! It is the ABC for the child. It is a staff for the weak; it is a sword for the strong. It is a true principle for the unity of the Church. It is like the eye of faith for the believer's soul.

May we learn to say it, believe it, truly confess it, and worthily live it.

1. What are the contents of our faith?
2. What is the origin and the division of the Apostles' Creed?
3. Is not "faith in Jesus" sufficient?
4. Is "believing the Gospel" a plain statement?
5. Does this creed belong to any one church?
6. Is our confession mental or experimental?
7. Discuss the statement: "no creed but the Bible"
8. Do you know this creed? believe it? confess it? live it?

## Three Distinct Persons

QUESTION 25 — *Since there is but one only divine essence, why speakest thou of Father, Son, and Holy Ghost?*

ANSWER — Because God has so revealed himself in his Word, that these three distinct persons are the one only true and eternal God.

●

From the fact that the Articles of our faith are readily divided into three parts: the first of God the Father and our creation; the second of God the Son, and our redemption; the third of God the Holy Ghost and our sanctification, this question is to the point. No, there are not three Gods: there is one only true and eternal God. Yet three distinct persons with three distinct properties are mentioned and we designate them by distinct names. That they nevertheless are *one,* is not a matter of speculation or imagination, but we believe in this *Trinity* "because God has so revealed himself in his Word." That answer is final and sufficient. By studying his Word, we learn concerning the Trinity:

1. *Its Unity.* These three are one. Hear, O Israel, the Lord thy God is one God. The three persons are one in Essence, so that each person has the complete divine Essence, and all the

divine attributes. God the Son has divine names, attributes, honor, and does divine work, such as creation (John 1:3). God the Holy Spirit is a divine person and not just a "good influence." For as a Person he speaks, prays, comforts, which a mere influence cannot do. God the Son is God, otherwise he cannot be our Saviour. God the Spirit is God, otherwise we cannot receive spiritual life and growth.

That these three are *one* is evident when we search the Scriptures.

The evidence is still: "Because God has so revealed himself." Beyond that we cannot, we need not, go.

2. *Its Mystery.* Even though the Trinity is no fleeting dream, we can no more explain it, than we can empty the ocean with a teaspoon, as Augustine learned. Analogies do not prove, but merely illustrate, its possibility. So we point to three lamps in one room which give not three, but one light. We think of ourselves as body, mind and soul. But the mystery remains. Do we understand or explain God? Do we know what Eternity means? Or do we really know the sun and the stars, or even a flower, or electricity, or the law of gravity, or even ourselves? Yet we may and must meditate upon the Trinity. "This is life eternal to know thee, the only true God," even though we know him in mystery. Art. IX of our Belgic Confession so comfortingly concludes concerning this mystery: "but we expect hereafter to enjoy the perfect knowledge and benefit thereof in heaven."

3. *Its Activity.* The Mohammedans kiss the Black Stone, the Kaba: their Alla is as dead as fatalism. In the Bible we learn that the Trinity is active internally. The Father generates the Son; the Son and the Holy Spirit proceed from the Father. The Holy Trinity is also active externally in creation, salvation and sanctification. These truths are some of the deep things of God. They are no child's play, and yet even a humble believer may reap a rich reward when he confesses them. As the Banner of the Church — rightly unfolded in Invocation, Doxology and Benediction — and as the Anchor of his soul it enables the believer to ride out the storms of Polytheism, Pantheism and Deism which find their climax in Atheism. Praise Father, Son and Holy Ghost!

1. What does **Trinity** mean?
2. If there are not evidences of the Trinity in nature, are there comparisons like light, man himself?

3. Do you believe that:
   All that we see of God is of God the Father?
   All that we know of God is of God the Son?
   All that we feel of God is of God the Holy Spirit?
4. In what does the Unity of the Trinity consist?
5. What is the distinction in the Trinity?
6. Prove that the three Persons are Persons.
7. Prove that the three Persons are God.
8. What is the threefold need of the Trinity for our salvation?

## God, the Father

QUESTION 26 — *What believest thou, when thou sayest, "I believe in God the Father Almighty, Maker of Heaven and Earth"?*

ANSWER — That the eternal Father of our Lord Jesus Christ (who of nothing made heaven and earth, with all that is in them; who likewise upholds and governs the same by his eternal counsel and providence) is, for the sake of Christ his Son, my God and my Father; on whom I rely so entirely, that I have no doubt, but he will provide me with all things necessary for soul and body: And further, that he will make whatever evils he sends upon me, in this valley of tears, turn out to my advantage; for he is able to do it, being Almighty God; and willing, being a faithful Father.

●

Here we learn how God, the Father, becomes God, *my* Father. The Fatherhood of God is a distinctly Christian and an exceedingly comforting doctrine. However, many who eloquently exalt the Fatherhood of God without a Scriptural basis are building on a wrong foundation, and their comfort is perverted and vain. Reasoning from the idea of their own fatherhood, they arrive at conclusions concerning God's Fatherhood. They would not punish their children severely and eternally, and now they think that God as Father will not do this either. But the Bible teaches us that we must begin with God's Fatherhood, and learn that our fatherhood is named after God's (Eph. 3:14-15). God was Father long before we became, or had, fathers. When we want to know the relation between God's Fatherhood and salvation we must know God the Father:

1. *As the Father of our Lord Jesus Christ.* Jesus is the Son of God. He is called the only begotten of the Father. "Thou art my Son; this day have I begotten thee." (Ps. 2:7). The Sonship of Christ is dealt with in Question 33. Here I confess that I believe in the Fatherhood of God in respect to Christ. He is the perfect Father, Eternal, not like us, temporal. He has no predecessor. The Son is always Son, not becoming Father.

Should one now ask how God, the Father of Christ, deals with sin, the answer is plain: Look at the Lamb of God — look at Calvary and the Cross!

2. *As the Father of Creation,* "who of nothing made Heaven and earth." He created matter, form and life. He undergirded his creation with laws — physical, moral and spiritual. He upholds this creation and governs it by his eternal counsel.

Should one now ask how God deals with sin as the Father of Creation he learns that every transgression meets with due reward. "Whatsoever a man soweth that shall he also reap." The laws of God are marvelous to the obedient, but they are retributive to the disobedient.

3. *As the Father of the believer.* "*My* Father," says the Catechism.

When we consider the Fatherhood of God in Christ and in Creation, we find little hope of comfort when that Fatherhood is applied to us in our natural, sinful estate. True, in Adam God is Father of mankind, Father by nature, but, having broken God's laws, we can only expect the justice which God established as the Father of Creation.

Now we come to the Christian view of God's Fatherhood when we learn that God the Father is, for the sake of Christ his Son, my God and *my* Father. Christ fulfilled the law for us. I must be the Lord's in life and death. From all eternity, through Bethlehem and Calvary, through his exaltation in Heaven, and his glorious return, the believer in Christ rightfully may call God "*my* Father." Temporal things are also seen in that light. Our needs will be supplied; whatever evils he sends in this valley of tears will "turn out to my advantage: for he is able to do it, being Almighty God; and willing, being a faithful Father."

That is what I confess when I say: I believe in God, the Father.

That is the way in which I name the Fatherhood of God.

That is the way in which I place my trust in God the Father, for Christ's sake, *my* Father.

1. Was God Father before the creation of man?
2. Can we claim God to be our Father without believing in the Sonship of Christ?
3. Why do you believe in Creation instead of Evolution?
4. Was there order in the creation as described in Genesis 1?
5. What is the meaning of the eternal generation of the Son?
6. Why is Christ called the only begotten Son?
7. How are we children by adoption?
8. What comfort does the Fatherhood of God bring to the adopted child of God?

## God's Providence

QUESTION 27 — *What dost thou mean by the Providence of God?*

ANSWER — The almighty and every where present power of God; whereby, as it were by his hand, he upholds and governs heaven, earth, and all creatures; so that herbs and grass, rain and drought, fruitful and barren years, meat and drink, health and sickness, riches and poverty, yea, and all things, come not by chance, but by his fatherly hand.

QUESTION 28 — *What advantage is it to us to know that God has created, and by his providence doth still uphold all things?*

ANSWER — That we may be patient in adversity, thankful in prosperity, and that in all things which may hereafter befall us, we place our firm trust in our faithful God and Father that nothing shall separate us from his love: since all creatures are so in his hand that without his will they can not so much as move.

●

The words "provide" and "providence" we met in the previous answer in connection with the Fatherhood of God. Here we learn that this providence is the almighty and everywhere present power of God to uphold and govern his creation.

To know this is a great advantage to the believer to be patient in adversity and to be thankful in prosperity, and to place his trust at all times in his faithful God and Father.

Providence means to see beforehand and the ability to bring it to pass. In him we live, move and have our being. Isaiah speaks of the stars: "He calleth them all by names"; and Jesus speaks of the hairs on our head. Abraham said: "The Lord will provide" (Gen. 22:34), and the Psalmist pictures God's Providence: "The eyes of all wait upon thee, and thou givest them their meat in due season." Everywhere in Scripture God's Providence is the firm trust of the believer that nothing shall separate him from God's love.

God did not leave his creation to itself or to another power, after he had created it. A jeweler may make a watch, wind it and then the watch may run without the maker. Not so in God's creation where "nothing happens without his appointment" (Art. XIII, Belgic Confession). If it were possible that God's Providence were removed for a single moment, this universe would plunge into chaos.

Men speak of *nature* as if it were a power apart from God. To be sure there are powerful forces in nature: forces of growth and of destruction, but nature's laws have no power apart from God: He made nature and gave nature its laws. We do not worship nature, but we worship God who made and maintains nature. It is wrong to speak of natural forces as if they had power apart from God, or even alongside of God, or in opposition to God. The wind and the waves obey his will.

*Luck,* or good or evil *Fortune,* is given credit or blamed by many who in the vicissitudes of life find no adequate reply to their questions when they turn from God. Tempting God's Providence in games and gambling is an evidence of lack of trust in our heavenly Father.

*Accidents,* or emphasis on *second causes,* as explanations of events beyond common expectations, is another way of by-passing God's Providence. In our common speech, perhaps it was an accident as far as our human mind is concerned: but for the Christian there is the assurance that all things come, not by chance, but by God's Fatherly hand.

*Fatalism* is the cold comfort people derive by grimly submitting to the inevitable. Fate is no power beyond God or equally strong as God. That ancient heathen idea of fatalism is often still found when we hear folks say: "It just had to be that way." Christianity knows no fatalism.

God's Providence is a fruitful source for meditation in connection with the use of means, when some wrongly refuse medicine or aid from a doctor in sickness; or in relation to the human will; or when we see the wicked prosper (Ps. 73). But God's child knows that all things work together for good to them that love God (Rom. 8:28). He knows it by revelation. And in that knowledge he places his trust in God when still he does not understand. Some time he will see face to face.

1. How is God's Providence evident in creation?
2. What is the distinction between Providence and Fatalism?
3. Does God's Providence oppose gambling?
4. Does Providence leave room for chance or luck?
5. May Christians cast lots to arrive at a decision?
6. What is the relation between Free Will and Providence; sin and Providence?
7. How do you account for natural laws and our faith in Providence?
8. What about the use of means and Providence?

## Jesus, That Is, a Saviour

QUESTION 29 — *Why is the Son of God called Jesus, that is, a Saviour?*

ANSWER — Because he saveth us, and delivereth us from our sins; and likewise, because we ought not to seek, neither can find salvation in any other.

QUESTION 30 — *Do such, then, believe in Jesus the only Saviour who seek their salvation and happiness of saints, of themselves, or any where else?*

ANSWER — They do not; for though they boast of him in words, yet in deeds they deny Jesus the only deliverer and Saviour; for one of these two things must be true, that either Jesus is not a complete Saviour; or that they, who by a true faith receive this Saviour, must find all things in him necessary to their salvation.

●

Jesus, precious name! Bernard said: the name Jesus is honey for the mouth, music for the ear, melody for the heart. It was given by the angel to both Joseph and Mary (Matt. 1:21 and Luke 1:31). It means the same as Joshua who led the Hebrews into the Promised land, while Moses, with the law, directed them to it. Likewise what the law could not do for us (Rom. 8:3) Jesus did for us by bringing us to Heaven. Jesus means "Saviour," for as the angel of the Lord predicted: "he shall save his people from their sins."

Ever since that pronouncement of the angel, attempts were made at an interpretation of the name and consequent work of Jesus. The Jews expected that Jesus would deliver them from

Rome, and were not so conscious of their need of their deliverance from sins. Ancient Church Councils spent much time in analyzing heresies concerning the humanity and divinity of Jesus, all reflecting upon the claim of the angel of Jesus as Saviour. Popular was the idea that Jesus was the link between God and man, and still many honor Jesus as the most wonderful example, a great Teacher. But all these eloquent phrases sink into insignificance compared to the angel's explanation: "Jesus, *for* he shall save his people from their sins." And Jesus himself confirmed this in his many statements, beginning with: "I am come that . . ."; or, "the Son of Man came to . . ."

If it becomes necessary to hold to the true interpretation of the name Jesus as Saviour from sins, it is even more difficult to persuade many concerning the words: "he shall save *his people.*" For there are many who agree to the truth indicated by the name Jesus as Saviour, but then make it universal in its application: for *all* people, and they point to I Tim. 2:6, "Who gave himself a ransom for all." Jesus' own words are, "For this is my blood in the new Testament which is shed for many for the remission of sins." (Matt. 26:28). The explanation is found in the two words translated by our English word *"for,"* the first meaning "on behalf of" and the second meaning "instead of." Another explanation is of value: "Sufficient for all — efficient for the believer."

Jesus is the all-sufficient and exclusive Saviour. The last part of answer 29 and the answer of question 30 are devoted to this all-important truth. We ought not to seek, neither can we find salvation in any other. "There is none other name under heaven given among men whereby we must be saved" (Acts 4:12). If we seek salvation and happiness of saints, or of ourselves, or anywhere else, we act as if Jesus were not a complete Saviour. They who receive Jesus by a true faith find all things in him necessary for their salvation.

Prayers to the saints find no example in the Bible. Jesus spoke with authority: "I am the way . . . Come unto me . . ." Symbolically the veil in the temple was rent so that we have free access unto the throne of grace. Peter calls the believers "an holy priesthood" (I Peter 2:5), and John writes in Rev. 1:6 that he "hath made us kings and priests," emphasizing the Priesthood of all believers. No, saints do not help us and we have no evidence that in intercession they are more favorably heard than the most

humble believer. If we do ask for the intercession of fellow believers, like the minister, or the Church, it is not asked because
they have more ready access to God, but on the basis of the communion of the saints.

### Is Jesus your Saviour?

1. How many names for Jesus can you find in the Bible?
2. Why are the names of Jesus important?
3. Was the name "Jesus" divinely given?
4. Who are "his people" whom he saves? Matt. 1:21.
5. What is the Hebrew equivalent for Jesus?
6. Mention Old Testament types of Jesus.
7. Why are we saved by his name? Acts 4:12.
8. Does the Bible teach prayers to saints, angels, or Mary, to obtain favors?

## Christ, That Is, Anointed

QUESTION 31 — *Why is he called Christ, that is, anointed?*

ANSWER — Because he is ordained of God the Father, and
anointed with the Holy Ghost, to be our chief Prophet and
Teacher; who has fully revealed to us the secret counsel and
will of God concerning our redemption: and to be our only
High Priest, who, by the one sacrifice of his body, has redeemed us, and makes continual intercession with the Father
for us; and also to be our eternal King, who governs us by
his Word and Spirit; and who defends and preserves us in (the
enjoyment of) that salvation he has purchased for us.

●

Jesus is a personal name; Christ is the title, or an official name.
His contemporaries knew Jesus and expected the Messiah, or
Christ. John the Baptist replied plainly to those who asked him,
"I am not the Christ." As time went on, the inner circle of disciples long in the dark were illuminated concerning Jesus, and Peter
gave utterance to what many had suspected: "Thou art the Christ,
the Son of the living God." (John 6:6). Now they confessed that
the Jesus whom they knew was the Messiah, the Christ, who was
promised. The words Messiah, Christ, and Anointed are all the
same words but in three different languages, namely Hebrew,
Greek and English, and they all have for their original meaning
the idea of "oil" which was the means of anointing.

Now why is Jesus called the Christ? We could say, because
he was the Messiah who was promised for ages. But then, how

would we know that someone else would not come after Jesus making similar claims? Hence we have the answer: because he is ordained of God the Father and anointed with the Holy Ghost. In anointing, the one who anoints is of the first importance: "No man taketh this honour unto himself" (Heb. 5:4). From all eternity God said: "Thou art my Son, this day have I begotten thee." And thrice from Heaven came the voice: "This is my beloved Son, hear ye him." The eternal value and the saving power of Christ depends upon this divine ordination. Surely Christ is our Saviour because of his own righteousness, but also because the Father sent him, and promised to receive his work instead of ours.

"And anointed with the Holy Ghost." In the announcement to Mary (Luke 1:36) and at the time of the baptism of Jesus we have evidence of that. Let us always remember the three Persons of the Trinity in connection with our salvation.

Now comes the question: Where unto was he anointed? Three distinct offices in the O. T. required anointing with oil for ordination: Prophet, Priest and King, and no one person could hold two of these offices in one person. But Christ was anointed unto all three: he is our Prophet and Priest and King.

The particular adjectives in connection with this threefold title are of the greatest importance in understanding the description of each office: Christ is our:

1. *Chief Prophet* (Deut. 18:5). Christ's great task of revealing the Father unto us is shown in the Gospels. And he sent his Spirit so that his revelation of God still comes to the heart of the hearer. There were and there are other prophets. When we confess the name of Christ we are such too. But among all those who speak for God, Christ is the *chief* Prophet. Hear ye him!

2. *Only High Priest.* Foreshadowed in Aaron (Ex. 30:30; see also Ps. 133:2). The Priest first sacrificed, then interceded for the people. The High Priest went into the Holy of Holies once a year to make reconciliation. Christ was both the sacrifice and the Priest. He went into the Holy of Holies on high showing his accomplished work. No other High Priest is needed today.

3. *Eternal King.* King David was Christ's type. But Kingship was temporal. Christ is the true King, and announced the coming of his Kingdom. He answered in the affirmative when Pilate asked, "Art thou a King then?" As King he has power: he said, "All power is given unto me." He governs us by his Word

and Spirit and defends and preserves us in the salvation he has purchased for us.

Truly he is called Christ. May we be taught by him, reconciled by him, and ruled by him. Then he is our Christ.

1. What is the meaning of the word Christ?
2. What is the significance of the fact that Christ was ordained of God the Father?
3. Where do you read of Christ's anointing?
4. To what three offices was Christ anointed?
5. What significant adjectives describe these offices?
6. What is the task of Christ as our chief Prophet and Teacher?
7. What is the task of Christ as our only High Priest?
8. What is the task of Christ as our eternal King?

## Partaker of His Anointing

QUESTION 32 — *But why art thou called a Christian?*

ANSWER — Because I am a member of Christ by faith, and thus am partaker of his anointing, that so I may confess his name, and present myself a living sacrifice of thankfulness to him; and also, that with a free and good conscience I may fight against sin and Satan in this life, and afterwards reign with him eternally, over all creatures.

●

"The disciples were called Christians first in Antioch" (Acts 11:26). They called themselves, "those of that way" or believers, or followers, or called. Perhaps it was given by way of ridicule as a nickname by those to whom the cross was foolishness, but it became a name of the most honorable implications.

There is perhaps no word in our language which is used so often and misused so frequently as the word Christian. We speak of Christian virtues, and of our Christian laws and that we are living in a Christian land. Whatever is commendable and good, whatever is in harmony with the highest ethical standard, is simultaneously said to be Christian.

But just because of its universal importance, this word is also frequently misused. We speak of our Christian era, but we hardly ever connect this year with the birth of Christ. We are living in a Christian community, but that does not indicate that all our neighbors are followers of Christ. So degenerate has its use become that it often expresses merely the contrast between it and barbarism. Are we called Christian for that reason?

In the brilliant setting of the confession concerning the Son of God his followers share the glory of his name, Christ, in being called Christian. Not after Jesus, like the Jesuits, are we called, for we are not little saviors. But we are called Christians, after Christ, the anointed, for we are partakers of his anointing, and somewhat share the honor and the activity of our Chief Priest, our only High Priest, and eternal King in so far as we too are: —

1. *Prophets* — "so that I may confess his name," the first requisite of open discipleship. To be sure, we do so when we make confession of faith, but also throughout our lives, and in every place (Matt. 10:32). As prophets we learn to confess, but also to spread his name; and evangelism and mission effort becomes the very heartbeat of the Christian.

2. *Priests* — "to present myself a living sacrifice of thankfulness to him" (Rom. 12:1). We are priests, for he "hath made us kings and priests unto God and the Father" (Rev. 1:6). We present ourselves sacrifices of thanksgiving, no bloody sacrifices, nor sacrifices for merit, but of gratitude. We view our finances that way, and also our services in the Lord's work, our talents of music and of teaching, much of which is given sacrificially. The minister is a priest in leading in worship, but so are all the members. When they are absent on the Lord's day from the Lord's house, what kind of priests are they?

3. *Kings* — "fight against sin and Satan, and reign with him." We fight the good fight of faith against our sins of thought, word and deed; against satanic evil, ignorance, unbelief and superstition, with the promise that afterwards we shall reign with Christ eternally over all creatures.

Partakers of his anointing. Christian — what a wonderful name, what a tremendous responsibility, what a glorious prospect! Why art thou called a Christian?

1. Where is the name Christian mentioned in the Bible?
2. How do we become Christians?
3. What does "partaker of his anointing" mean?
4. By what figures of speech does the Bible present the mystical union between Christ and the Christians?
5. Do we preach Christ or the Christian?
6. What is our task as Prophet?
7. What is our task as Priest?
8. What is our task as King?

# His Only Begotten Son

QUESTION 33 — *Why is Christ called the only begotten Son of God, since we are also the children of God?*

ANSWER — Because Christ alone is the eternal and natural Son of God; but we are children adopted of God, by grace, for his sake.

●

"All men are sons of God," is a statement that contains a grain of truth and a mountain of heresy. In the sense of creation, men in their natural estate, and even the angels, are sons of God. But we have become children of wrath, so that brings no comfort or happiness.

Only by grace, through the blood of Christ, do natural men become adopted children of God. Therein is our salvation and joy.

Having grasped this distinction, there is still the possibility that the Sonship of Christ and the adoption of the believer are placed on the same level. Throughout the history of the Church men have tried to humanize Christ to the level of men, or to deify men to the stature of Christ.

Now our attention is called to the sharp dividing-line between the two.

I. Jesus Christ is:

    a. God's only Son. In the announcement to Mary he is called "Son of God" (Luke 1:35). In his baptism there was a voice, "This is my beloved Son"; and Jesus' favorite name was "Son of Man" to express the fact that he was Son of God.

    b. God's only-begotten Son. Many omit "begotten" from the creed. But the Bible contains this expression many times (John 1:14, John 3:16; I John 4:9). "Begotten," as learned from Psalm 2, means the eternal generation of the Son, never ending; the Son always Son and the Father always Father. When born in Bethlehem he did not become the Son of God: "Before Abraham was, I am." This is a great mystery of the 1st and 2nd Persons of the Trinity, not to be understood or explained by us but revealed in God's Word and to be believed.

    c. Jesus is God, co-essential and co-eternal with the Father (Belgic Conf. X).

II. The Believer is:

    a. God's son (Rom. 8:14) from the moment of his conversion, thus from a certain time, not like Jesus from eternity. The element of eternity for the believer is found in the pre-destination of God's council, and in the expectation of continuance. But there was a time when he was not a son of God, which cannot be said of Jesus.

    b. God's adopted son. If the eternal generation of the Son is beyond our comprehension, our regeneration is also a mystery. Adoption in the council of God is before our re-generation, but for us the two are the same. Adoption is mentioned, because we are speaking in terms of Father and child (Gal. 4:5).

    c. God's son by grace, for Christ's sake. Unmerited love for the sinner and Christ's precious blood made, from the sinner, the son.

And for what purpose did we embark upon this tumultuous sea of theological difficulty, when the storm well-nigh overwhelmed the little bark of our finite mind, when at times the waves lifted us high, and then again plunged us into the depths of mental agony when words fail?

The chasm of separation between the deity of Christ and the humanity of the believer can never be bridged. But God's intent is to re-unite the believer to that Christ who is God, and as such can save us by grace, for his sake. That is the never-ending marvel of it all.

1. What was Jesus' question in regard to his sonship? Matt. 22:42.
2. What was Jesus' approval in reply to Peter's statement about his sonship? Matt. 16:16.
3. Is not Christ's threefold office sufficient without his sonship?
4. What is the effect of the "eternal and natural Son of God" upon our salvation?
5. What is the distinction between the sonship of Christ and the sonship of the believer?
6. Are all men sons of God?
7. How do we become adopted children?
8. What are some of the evidences of our sonship? Rom. 8:14, 15, 16.

# Our Lord

QUESTION 34 — *Wherefore callest thou him "our Lord"?*

ANSWER — Because he hath redeemed us, both soul and body, from all our sins, not with gold or silver, but with his precious blood; and hath delivered us from all the power of the devil; and thus hath made us his own property.

●

The Confession of the Church still states: I believe in Jesus Christ, his only begotten Son, *our Lord*. In practice both pulpit and pew read: I believe in Jesus Christ, his only begotten Son, *our Saviour*.

The young convert is asked: Do you believe in Jesus Christ as your Saviour? Seldom the question is added: Do you surrender your soul and body to *your Lord?* The new disciple needs much guidance in this direction. When this is lacking or minimized he does not practice his religion in every area of life, and has little joy and less enthusiasm in his discipleship.

And when older Christians neglect this truth, even though their feet are on the way to Zoar, their affection is still in Sodom. Witness their lack of moral conviction, their spiritual indifference, their unwillingness to obey God's will in business and pleasure and vocation. They are sure that Christ is on their side; but are they on Christ's side? That is all-important. And that is the issue in confessing Christ as *our Lord* (Acts 2:36, I Cor. 12:3).

As second Person in the Trinity Christ is Lord from eternity. As our Mediator he became Lord.

1. *In redemption.* "Because he hath redeemed us." In the Old Testament the first born, property and slaves, were redeemed, that is, bought back (Lev. 25:27, Neh. 5:8). We are redeemed, bought back, from all our sins, but not with gold or silver. We are redeemed, body and soul, by Christ's precious blood (I Pet. 1:18). First we belonged to sin; now we belong to Christ. Whether we live or die *we are the Lord's* (Rom. 14:8).

2. *Deliverance* from all power of the devil. Temptations lose their power to overcome us; in fact, so much so, that what were real temptations before are temptations no more. We do

not steal even though the opportunity is present, for we know that God does not want us to do this. And so it is in all of our life. The more we find that these temptations have no appeal for us, the more we are freed from the power of the devil. The Holy Spirit sent by Christ enables us. The power of the devil may be great; Christ's power is greater.

3. *In Ownership.* "And has made us his own property." Escaping the powers of evil is good, but now we are the servants of a new Master and we heed his commandments; that is essential. Obedience to his will, dedication of our time and talents and possessions to the Lord's cause now becomes the inevitable result. We belong to him, body and soul, and all the activities and possibilities of both body and soul are at his command. First we heard his invitation: "Come unto me." Now we obey his commandment: "Go ye into all the world." That includes a surrender of our entire being; the humblest task we do as unto the Lord. It means that we look at every activity in the entire sphere of our life through the sanctified glasses of Kingdom interest and growth.

"But to us there is but one God, the Father, of whom are all things, and we in him; and one Lord Jesus Christ, by whom are all things, and we by him" (I Cor. 8:6). We love that New Testament name: Our Lord Jesus Christ. And we pray for grace to be true to our Confession: And in Jesus Christ, his only begotten Son, *our Lord.*

1. In the Old Testament the triune God is called Lord as Sovereign of his creation. Is Christ "our Lord" in the same way?
2. Name the threefold activity in which Christ engaged to be our Lord.
3. Does obedience to our Lord refer to spiritual obedience only?
4. With what did Christ redeem us to be our Lord?
5. What kind of obedience should a Christian render to his Lord?
6. What comfort does the Christian derive in temptation when he is the Lord's?
7. From what are we delivered when we are the Lord's?

## Conceived — Born

QUESTION 35 — *What is the meaning of these words, "He was conceived by the Holy Ghost, born of the Virgin Mary"?*

ANSWER — That God's eternal Son, who is and continueth true and eternal God, took upon him the very nature of man, of the flesh and blood of the Virgin Mary, by the operation of the Holy Ghost; that he might also be the true seed of David like unto his brethren in all things, sin excepted.

QUESTION 36 — *What profit dost thou receive by Christ's holy conception and nativity?*

ANSWER — That he is our Mediator; and with his innocence and perfect holiness, covers, in the sight of God, my sins, wherein I was conceived and brought forth.

●

Great is the mystery of godliness: "God was manifested in the flesh" (I Tim. 3:16). The mystery of the State of Humiliation! In the Advent season ours is the joy of the Angel's announcement, the music of the heavenly host, the ecstasy of the shepherds; the star in the East, a Babe in the manger, and a mother's low prayer. And well we may be joyful, for Bethlehem's stable is still the hope of the world! Little do we think of the price that was paid! For us it is a mystery of joy: for Christ it was the mystery of Humiliation. No, we cannot fathom that mystery, even our words will fail, but our faith will express itself in amazement, as we trace the Biblical picture of our Saviour's birth in that he was:

1. *Conceived by the Holy Ghost.* Unto Mary first this marvel was revealed: "The Holy Ghost shall come upon thee, and the power of the Highest shall overshadow thee" (Luke 1:35). But Joseph was concerned too, and he was informed: "For that which is conceived in her is of the Holy Ghost" (Matt. 1:20). Now by the creative power of the Holy Spirit, a holy, human nature was created, which could bear the sin of our defiled human nature. Conceived *by* the Holy Ghost, not from, or derived from the Holy Spirit, but caused by the Holy Spirit. If the birth of a human being is wonderful when we think of body and soul in its beginning and derivation, here we have the greatest miracle through a creative act of the Holy Spirit! So Christ, who knew no sin, did not share Adam's guilt and pollution.

2. *Born of the Virgin Mary.* "Be it unto me according to thy word" (Luke 1:38) were the words of Mary's consent. Through her the promises unto David were fulfilled, and in David, born of Jewish and Moabitish ancestors, all humanity has a share when Jesus was born of the flesh and blood of the Virgin. Mary remained a virgin in the birth of Christ whose conception was sinless, because the Holy Ghost overshadowed her, not because she was sinless, as Roman Catholicism maintains. To maintain that Mary was sinless has no Biblical basis (Luke 1:47). The miracle of her immaculate conception would be removed just one generation, for how were her parents without sin? Mary was blessed among women, but needed a Saviour. For us, the expression "immaculate conception" refers to Christ, not to Mary. The Virgin Birth honors Mary but does not entitle her to be worshiped. That belongs to Christ.

3. *Continued in His Deity.* He is and continueth true and eternal God in his Incarnation. He became like unto his brethren, sin excepted, and he remained God when he took upon himself the very nature of man. Thus we speak of the two natures of Christ, divine and human. His divinity is not changed into humanity; his divinity is not lost in his humanity. His human and divine natures are not intermingled into a new nature. There is no division or separation of two natures in one Person.

What profit do we receive from these mysteries? That Christ is our Mediator, not only when he died for our actual sins on the cross, but when the original sin and guilt, wherein *we* were conceived and born, is covered by his innocence and perfect holiness, from the moment *he* was conceived by the Holy Ghost, born of the Virgin Mary. The birth of Christ makes us mindful of our own. From the moment of our birth till our death, Christ is our complete and perfect Saviour!

1. What are the two states of our Mediator?
2. What are the five steps in the state of Humiliation?
3. What do you mean by the Incarnation?
4. What is the mystery of the Conception?
5. Whose immaculate conception do we acknowledge, that of Jesus or of Mary?
6. Is faith in the Virgin Birth essential to our salvation?
7. What do the two genealogies in Matthew and Luke teach concerning the "seed of David"?
8. What is the relation between Christ's sinless conception and our sinful conception?
9. Mention prophecies concerning Christ's birth.

# He Suffered

QUESTION 37 — *What dost thou understand by the words, "He suffered"?*

ANNSWER — That he, all the time he lived on earth, but especially at the end of his life, sustained in body and soul, the wrath of God against the sins of all mankind, that so by his passion, as the only propitiatory sacrifice, he might redeem our body and soul from everlasting damnation, and obtain for us the favor of God, righteousness and eternal life.

●

Our generation, bowed by the world's sorrow, questions the Scriptural significance of our faith when we confess concerning our Lord Jesus Christ: He suffered. We too, they say, suffered, and even more so. We have suffered in cities turned to rubble, armies annihilated, races obliterated. We have witnessed the atrocities of liquidation, the demolition of Murder Inc., the ghettos, Death March, Lidice, and the D. P.'s. We know the millions dying of famine in India; the dispossessed in Korea. The dead and dying on battlefields and in hospitals cry out: We too have suffered! Can you still preach the suffering of the pale Galilean? he, who lived a tranquil life in primitive Palestine? True, he hungered and thirsted; He wept at Lazarus' grave; He had no place where to lay his head; a sad fate sent him to an untimely death. But why in the face of all humanity's misery do you still confess so insistently: *"He* suffered"? And what does it avail?

Deep shafts are sunk into the infinite truth of God to furnish the reply: 1. *That he* . . . and we have learned who *he* is: in one person very God and real, righteous man. His suffering was infinite because he is very God. His divine nature enabled him to bear in his human suffering what no man can or did bear: "the wrath of God against the sins of all mankind." I John 1 :7 emphasizes this truth: "The blood of Jesus Christ, *his Son,* cleanses us from all sin." Belgic Confession 21. 2. *All the time he lived on earth.* Surely, Gethsemane and Calvary reveal the steps of his Humiliation. But they did not begin there. His Virgin Birth; his becoming like us, sin excepted; his surrender of his heavenly glory to live in a sin-cursed world; his miracles which were attributed to Be-elzebub and his teachings which were pronounced blasphemy — these and more were parts of his suffering concerning which we catch a faint glimpse in his prayer: "Father, glorify me with the glory I had with thee, before the world began" (John 17:5). Jesus emptied himself of that glory. And no one can gauge the depth of misery when in contrast to that glory he cried: "My God, My God, why hast thou forsaken me?" 3. *That he might redeem our body and soul from everlasting damnation.* His passion furnished the only propitiatory sacrifice. So he suffered in his Offices as Prophet, Priest and King, in body and soul. "And with his stripes we are healed." Canons of Dort II, 3. 4. *To obtain for us the favor of God, righteousness and eternal life.* In the Incarnation he brings God to man; in his suffering he brings man to God. "For Christ also has once suffered for our sins, the just for the unjust, that he might bring us to God" (I Peter 3:18.) That is why we still amazingly confess: *He suffered.*

1. Quote prophecies concerning Christ's suffering.
2. When did Christ suffer?
3. For whom did Christ suffer?
4. Did Christ suffer in body and soul?
5. What did his deity add to his suffering?
6. How many descriptive terms of Christ's suffering, like sacrifice, atonement, do you find in the Bible?
7. Is it necessary to believe that Christ's suffering was substitutionary?
8. What do you believe when we speak of limited atonement?

# Under Pontius Pilate

QUESTION 38 — *Why did he suffer under Pontius Pilate, as his judge?*

ANSWER — That he, being innocent, and yet condemned by a temporal judge, might thereby free us from the severe judgment of God, to which we were exposed.

●

Wherever the banners of Christianity are unfolded, there always will be a moment of hesitation when we come to this hiatus in our Confession. Here we stand by the deep chasm in the description of Christ: "Born of the Virgin Mary, suffered under Pontius Pilate," omitting his youth, life, words, miracles, which we consider so important.

One answer to that at least might be that the Creed permits no final interpretation of Christianity as being the good life or a mere norm of morality. Christ's life was admirable, his teachings unsurpassable, but it was his suffering that brings atonement with God, from which at-one-ment with humanity flows.

But why even mention Pontius Pilate? Why honor him by being mentioned in the same breath with the Holy Ghost and with Mary? Or why should history's finger be pointed at him as the cause of the world's darkest day? Why not Annas, or Caiaphas, or Judas, or the Jewish people, whom the ignorant still defy as "Christ killers"?

It is not our purpose to defend or amend the Creed. But it will add another dimension to our appreciation of Jesus' sacrifice when we consider that he suffered *under Pontius Pilate*. This part of our Confession is essential: 1. For its *historical value*. Pontius Pilate was Governor over Judea from A. D. 26-36. He was born during the reign of Emperor Augustus and ruled under Emperor Tiberius. Pilate was the judge of Christ, that is a matter of historic record, not a figment of foolish faith or imagination. The custom was to mention the name of the ruler to record the event. Isaiah had his vision in the year when King Uzziah died. Joseph was taxed when Cyrenius was Governor of Syria. Even the unbeliever must believe in Christ's trial before Pilate, as a matter of history. 2. As a *prophetic fulfillment*. The dying patriarch Jacob prophesied that "the sceptre shall not depart from Judah, nor a lawgiver from between his feet, till Shiloh come" (Gen. 49:10). So the Jewish rulers Annas and Caiaphas in their self-appointed investigation had to submit and defer to the Roman government. God's word was fulfilled. 3. As a *legal confirmation*. Roman law and authority were under God, as Jesus said to Pilate: "Thou couldest have no power at all against me, except it were given thee from above" (John 19:10). Hence the verdict of authority is the verdict of God. So Jesus could not die the death of a martyr to be our Saviour. He could not die of hunger in the wilderness; the sea could not overwhelm him. No, his death must be legal, for we are under legal condemnation. Christ is our divinely recognized legal propitiation in that he suffered *under Pontius Pilate,* "to free us from the severe judgment of God." Synod of Dort II, 7. 4. As a Testimonial *of his innocency*. Three times Pilate confessed: "I find no fault in him" (Luke 23:22). "I find no cause of death in him." Belgic Confession 21. His innocency was pronounced by Pilate in his official capacity. Thus we are reminded that he suffered not for his sin, but for us. Such a Saviour we need. Glory to God, such a Saviour we have!

1. Name the three trials of Jesus before religious courts.
2. Name the three trials of Jesus before civil courts.
3. Mention illegal procedures in them.
4. Who testified to Jesus' innocence?
5. Why is Pontius Pilate singled out in the creed?
6. Explain that the suffering of Jesus was voluntary, vicarious, and victorious.
7. Did Jesus suffer in his divine nature?
8. How are we freed from the severe judgment of God?

## The Cross and the Curse

QUESTION 39 — *Is there anything more in his being crucified, than if he had died some other death?*

ANSWER — Yes, there is, for thereby I am assured, that he took on him the curse which lay upon me; for the death of the cross was accursed of God.

●

Popular conception, which glorifies and venerates the symbol of the Cross, suffers a tremendous shock in this stern, Biblical presentation of the Cross as the curse of God.

What is our first reaction, when the crucifixion of Christ is commemorated in meditation, or presented in a visible Cross, as the symbol of Christianity?

Some see in the Cross "the emblem of suffering and shame" and weep for Jesus in sympathetic attitude like the daughters of Jerusalem. Others eulogize it as the universally accepted symbol of Faith Triumphant, Hope Eternal, Love Immortal and Service Sacrificial. In the Church we place a golden imitation upon the altar or the communion table. There we carve it in stone and etch it in multitudinous forms on our Gothic windows. Its distinctive position on the steeple is indicative of our faith that it "towers o'er the wrecks of time." Diamond-studded it is worn around the neck and adorns the lapel. Wherever we wish to create a religious atmosphere or describe an influence of whatever is decent, moral, sacrificial — the Red Cross, the Blue Cross — this symbol is flaunted to the sky in the name of all that is benevolent and philanthropic.

And much of that we appreciate and gladly share. But **the** point is, that many willfully neglect the basic issue, and have lost the true significance of the symbol. Symbols are silent witnesses. Their interpretation is mainly subjective, and hence partial and inaccurate.

But *living* words proclaim the ever living truth. So we cling to the *living* Word of God for the true meaning of Calvary. Our Catechism steers us in that safe but ofttimes undesired course. Over against all popular conceptions we stand face to face with this stern reality, which no flowery eloquence nor poetic fancy can hide: the *cross* is the sign of *God's curse!*

The curse of God! Not merely as man curses in an evil moment without the power to carry out his threat! But God's curse upon mankind because of sin is positive in its power and universal in its application. It brings thorns and thistles, sickness and death, and even though restrained by God's common grace, ultimately culminates in eternal damnation (Galatians 3:10).

Now crucifixion was the death of one accursed: "Cursed is every one that hangeth on a tree." Stephen was stoned, James was beheaded, but Christ was crucified. So it is stated in our Communion Liturgy: "That he took upon himself the curse due to us, that he might fill us with his blessing." So the Canons of Dort teach (II-4). "He bore the wrath of God and the curse of God." So our Catechism asks: "Is there anything more in his being crucified?" and in the answer points to the curse of God. Galatians 3:13: "Christ has redeemed us from the curse of the law, being made a curse for us." That is centric and fundamental; all other interpretations are peripheral and circumstantial. That is the Christian's glory as he takes the "shadow of the Cross for his abiding place."

1. Why was crucifixion necessary in relation to prophecy?
2. Why was crucifixion necessary in relation to our curse?
3. Whence is our curse?
4. How did Christ take our curse?
5. Name supernatural events during the crucifixion.
6. What does the Bible mean by the blood of Christ?
7. What is glorying in the cross of Christ?
8. What is carrying our cross?
9. What are the seven sayings of Jesus while he was on the cross?

# Even Unto Death

QUESTION 40 — *Why was it necessary for Christ to humble himself even unto death?*

ANSWER — Because with respect to the justice and truth of God, satisfaction for our sins could be made no otherwise, than by the death of the Son of God.

●

Of all the steps of Christ's humiliation, his death is especially mentioned as such in the Word of God: Phil. 2:8. He humbled himself and became obedient unto death.

Christian people believe that Christ died that they might live, but that fact is observed more by way of intimation than by actual contemplation. When we enlarge upon the details of Christ's suffering and then neglect the climax of it all, the question: Why was it necessary for Christ to die? is most essential.

Deep emotion stirs our soul, and our hearts are strangely warmed when we sing of "the blood of the Crucified One." But when he said: "It is finished," why did he not descend from the cross and claim his Kingdom? We are moved with compassion when we walk again the Via Dolorosa or painfully consider the betrayal and the agony in the Garden. We see him carrying the cross, we shudder at his stripes, the crown of thorns, the nail-scarred hands and feet. On Good Friday, the day of his death, we dwell upon the Seven Sayings, but the following 36 hours of silence are silent indeed. Even at Communion we mostly speak of Love, Faith, Sacrifice, Self-examination, all good subjects, but always shrinking from considering at any length the reason for his death.

Well may our hearts be touched by what our Saviour suffered. But even though not so appealing to our sympathy or sentiment, here we must learn that satisfaction for our sin demanded the death of Christ, with respect to —

1. *God's Justice.* Not as a mere objective admission of God's justice but as a personal recognition of God's right to establish the standard of good and evil. This our first Adam claimed to be his right. Robbing God of that right was a sin against God's justice and worthy of death. Now God's justice is demonstrated and again vindicated in the death of our second Adam, our substitute.

2. *God's Truth*. Man denied the truth of God, when he listened to the instigation of the devil and disregarded God's warning: Gen. 2:17, "Thou shalt not eat of it." Death was the penalty. But Jesus said: "I come to do thy will, O God," and in the voluntary death of him who said: "I am the truth," the truth of God is established in heaven and hell and all the world. Belgic Confession 20. Hence all false distinctions between the two Persons of the Godhead, that speak of the loving Jesus and the cruel Old Testament deity, are hereby silenced. Now our death is not a satisfaction for our sins, but only an abolishing of sin, and a passage into eternal life. (Question 42)

The death of Christ has serious warnings. Since Christ died, all who go about establishing their own code of morals apart from revelation, sin against God's justice, and all who do not accept Christ's truth make God a liar (I John 5:10).

The death of Christ has great blessings for the believer. That will be our never-ending theme of praise for Christ who satisfied God's justice and truth in his voluntary, vicarious and victorious death.

1. Why did the Justice of God demand the death of Christ?
2. What is the relation between the Truth of God and Christ's death?
3. Was, then, the love of God not in evidence at Christ's death?
4. Where was death threatened to the sinner?
5. Why is Christ's death a satisfaction for our sins?
6. Why should we meditate upon Christ's death as well as his suffering?
7. Where was Christ's death prophesied?
8. What events testified concerning his death?
9. What happened when Christ died?

## Low in the Grave

QUESTION 41 — *Why was he also "buried"?*

ANSWER — Thereby to prove that he was really dead.

●

Not in a potter's field, but in a rich man's family tomb, a new rock-hewn sepulcher, in a garden, sealed with a stone, guarded by soldiers, the body of Jesus was laid. Two considerate friends thus fulfilled divine prophecy concerning him whom they secretly loved while he lived and now at his death significantly honored.

Come, see the place where they laid him. Think of Nicodemus and Joseph who rendered this belated service. Meditate upon the women who came when the disciples fled. But think most of all of him: his nail-pierced hands no longer extended in blessing and healing; his feet no longer carrying him about doing good; that voice is silent now; that loving heart no longer beats. Think of him who raised Lazarus, and ask once more: "Why was he also buried?"

Cold, formal and disappointing is the answer here given:

1. *To prove that he was really dead.* This answer can never be rated among the great teachings in our Heidelberg Catechism. We knew that he died *before* his burial. Sacred Scripture states explicitly: He gave up the ghost. Roman officials knew it; no one was taken from the cross alive. The soldiers knew it, when they pierced his side. The friends knew it, who claimed his body. His burial was not required to prove his death.

Yet there is some value in this answer: in his burial there was no possibility of mistaken identity in the coming resurrection.

But Ursinus himself gives two additional reasons in the explanation of his own Catechism. These we gladly add. Why was he also buried?

2. *For Christ's humiliation.* Jesus suffered this for us too. The curse of sin included: "Dust thou art, and unto dust thou shalt return." Jesus' sinless body was thus humiliated to the extent of his burial. Yet true it was of him: Psalm 16:10: "Thou shalt not suffer thy holy one to see corruption." And when we face the difficulty of his two natures in connection with his humiliation in the grave, Belgic Confession 19 states that even in the grave his divine nature remained united with his human nature.

3. *To sanctify our grave.* When Joseph faced death, he must have found comfort in the thought that he would be laid where Jesus lay and rose from the dead. That is our comfort too. No flowery wreath, no marble mausoleum, no human effort to make our burial places appear like beautiful parks can hide the ugly fact of the grave. But Jesus was buried. He sanctified the grave for us. He promised: I live and ye shall live also. Then for the Christian the burial place becomes God's Acre. Then when we lower the bodies of our beloved dead, we are comforted in the believer's committal: "O grave where is thy victory? But thanks be to God, who giveth us the victory through our Lord Jesus Christ."

"Low in the grave he lay, Jesus my Lord." Comfort and hope come to the believer, when through Christ our grave is but a portal which after the darkness of death opens to life, and life eternal. Come, see the place where they laid him!

1. Who provided for Christ's burial?
2. What acts preparatory to burial proved that Christ's death was real?
3. Does the reality of Christ's death have a bearing on the Resurrection?
4. How does Christ's burial comfort us when we bury believers?
5. If Christ died for us, why must we die?
6. Is our death a passage, a door, into life eternal?
7. Which step in Humiliation was Christ's burial?
8. Did Jesus prophesy concerning his own burial?

## Why Must We Also Die?

QUESTION 42 — *Since, then, Christ died for us, why must we also die?*

ANSWER — Our death is not a satisfaction for our sins, but only an abolishing of sin and a passage into eternal life.

●

Penetrating and straight as an arrow shot from a bow this question comes home to our heart in the hour of our sorrow: Christ died for us; why, then, must we also die?

Was not Enoch translated and Elijah taken up? Might there not be a visible distinction between the believer and the unbeliever when we come to the end of our earthly journey? And is not the promise at Jesus' coming in I Cor. 15:51, "We shall not all sleep"; and in I Thess. 4:17, "Then we who are alive and remain shall be caught up with them in the clouds, to meet the Lord in the air"? Why, then, must *we* die?

Perhaps this question runs parallel with the question why a Christian is not translated and glorified at the moment of his conversion. However, when Jesus departed he said: "I pray not that thou shouldest take them out of the world" (John 17:15). Hence it is not as Martha said: "If thou hadst been here, my brother would not have died"; for he is with us. Whether we live or whether we die, we are the Lord's.

Removing the scaffolding of an earthly Christian life, we behold God's perfected building in a Christian's death. That death is:

(I) *Not a satisfaction for our sins.* Death is our enemy, our last enemy, our conquered enemy, but still our enemy; and neither flowers nor eloquence, nor marble monuments, nor "animated bust" can hide our grief. Jesus wept at Lazarus' grave. And death is real; death is separation from our loved ones. And separation means sorrow. The philosophical denial of reality: "There is no death, what seems so is transition," brings no comfort and is not true. True Christian comfort is found in the fact that Christ died for our transgressions, that our death is no satisfaction for our sins; and that therefore there is no separation from Christ "who died for us, that whether we wake or sleep, we should live together with him" (I Thess. 5:10). That, first of all, takes the sting from death. We can be satisfied with that.

(II) *A dying unto sin.* Not dying for sin, Jesus did that. But dying unto sin is a Christian's life-long struggle, and only death can end that struggle. For our bodies are brakes on the wheels on the road to perfection. We are not free from the presence of sin, as long as the eye-gate and the ear-gate and physical desires dominate our spiritual aspiration. Our sin is a burden to us, and with Paul we cry out; "Miserable man that I am, who shall deliver me from the body of this death?" Now death sets us free from sin's presence as well as from sin's power and sin's penalty. To be free from sin, O glorious prospect! But death is needed for that, and that is one answer as to why we must die.

(III) *Entering into life eternal.* We deserved spiritual death, separation from God, but at death we receive eternal life, true communion with God. Now those who did not and those who will not sleep cannot take this imperfect body with them. "We shall not all sleep, but we shall all be changed." "Flesh and blood cannot inherit the kingdom of God," so some change, we cannot tell how, must come to them too. And for the believers who do sleep, no spiritual death as part of the curse awaits them, but eternal life as the crown of salvation. That is no defeat, but "death is swallowed up in victory. . . when this mortal shall have put on immortality." The Christian believes in Christ's resurrection and receives Christ's promise: "where I am, ye shall be also." Blessed life eternal is now in its realization and completion.

No wonder we can now say with the Apostle: "O death, where

is thy sting?" For such a death is no condemnation but a coronation; it is not defeat but victory; it is not loss but gain. Death opens wide the gates of life eternal. We do not stand mute and helpless when this troublesome question confronts us. "Thanks be to God who giveth us the victory through our Lord Jesus Christ." I Cor. 15:57.

1. Who did not die in the O. T. dispensation?
2. Who will not die in the N. T. dispensation?
3. What changes were necessary for them?
4. Why is death our enemy?
5. Mention three reasons for our death.
6. What is dying unto sin?
7. Explain the presence, penalty and power of sin in relation to death.
8. How is death gain for the believer?

## By Virtue Thereof

QUESTION 43 — *What further benefit do we receive from the sacrifice and death of Christ on the Cross?*

ANSWER — That, by virtue thereof, our old man is crucified, dead and buried with him: that so the corrupt inclinations of the flesh may no more reign in us; but that we may offer ourselves unto him a sacrifice of thanksgiving.

●

Jesus' work of salvation is one in its conception and completion: He is a perfect Saviour. Jesus' death removed the curse of the law. Here a further benefit is stated, that he also fulfilled the demands of the law. By virtue of the Cross, by its power, we die unto sin and live unto holiness.

This is entirely misinterpreted by Arminian-minded believers, and often misunderstood by many who hold the Calvinistic Confession. Their common error is that since Jesus died for their justification, it is now optional to accept or to refuse this offer, and to work out their own sanctification. However, here we are instructed that Christ's salvation is one and complete. Sanctification is by the Cross too!

*By virtue thereof,* that is, by its power, not by our wish or will, our old man is crucified, dead and buried!

The power of the Cross unto sanctification! How few give credit or consideration to this work of our Saviour! They sing of pardoning grace, they walk with him in the garden; they glory in the Cross and testify of the cleansing blood, but rarely do they feel the need of sanctifying grace! They sail the ocean of "Redemption, full and free," and hoist the banner of the Cross. Then they nail the flag of good works and pious devotion to the mast-head. In their Christian zeal the Cross is almost forgotten and becomes a mere ballast in the ship. Yes, we must wait in Jerusalem for the Holy Spirit, but in our haste to take up our multiplied Christian activities, we forget even that. Now "it is up to us."

But loyal to God's Word, this answer lifts the Cross on high! Higher than the flag of law, obedience and good works, high above our ideas of choice or doubt whether the new life will result, and whether and to what extent the new life will be evident. Here again we are led away from self to the Cross!

*By virtue thereof,* comes the power to will and to work. By virtue thereof, we are constrained to do his will. By virtue thereof, we feel the power of inner persuasion against the corrupt inclinations of the flesh. By virtue thereof, we say after Paul: "I am crucified with Christ; it is no longer I that live, but Christ liveth in me": in our heart; in our reason; in our will; in our positive action and negative restraint.

So we merit Jesus' word: "Now ye are clean," John 15:3, and the Apostle's epithet: "Holy Brethren," Hebrews 3:1. And when then our Communion Liturgy states "that we are in the midst of death," we know that we are not free from sin till our parting breath, but that our perfection is in Christ. *In him* we are more than conquerors. His Cross enables us to gain the victory. The old man is crucified, dead and buried. That too is his work in us and through us that we may offer ourselves a sacrifice of thanksgiving.

1. Is the benefit of Christ's death limited to our justification?
2. How does the death of Christ urge us to sanctification?
3. How is our "old man crucified, dead and buried with him"?
4. What is the relation between Christ's death and our offer of Thanksgiving?
5. Does obedience to the law now become a Christian's delight?
6. Does the death of Christ furnish motive power for all Christian endeavor?
7. Is the Cross then a mere historic fact or a present inspiration?
8. What assurance is promised in Romans 8:32?

# He Descended Into Hell

QUESTION 44 — *Why is there added, "He descended into hell"?*

ANSWER — That in my greatest temptations, I may be assured, and wholly comfort myself in this, that my Lord Jesus Christ, by his inexpressible anguish, pains, terrors and hellish agonies, in which he was plunged during all his sufferings, but especially on the cross, hath delivered me from the anguish and torments of hell.

●

We of the Reformed persuasion are exceedingly thankful for the catechetical instruction of this part of the Apostles' Creed.

Many who with us accept and confess this creed embark upon a sea of such odd, unbiblical and even fantastic interpretations, that it would seem, like some falsely proclaim, that faith is believing what you know is not true.

Some have changed the word "hell" to "hades," or the grave — but we already confessed: "he was buried"; that would be useless duplication. Being offended at the "impolite terminology," others have scratched this phrase from their liturgical confession, and so have shipwrecked the ecumenicity of the creed. To speak of Limbo Patrum — like the Roman Catholics hold — to save the Old Testament saints, is to contradict the general teaching of the Bible concerning the dead. Lutherans interpret it to mean that Jesus fought the devil. But they forget Jesus' word: "It is finished," and they also make this phrase the first step in exaltation while it evidently refers to Jesus' humiliation. To say that it refers to Jesus' preaching in hell, especially for those who perished in Noah's flood, is to forget that death is the end of grace. Turning away from all these, we learn that this article is a distinct expression of our faith that —

1. *Jesus suffered the pains of hell,* during all his suffering, but especially on the cross, when he said: "My God, my God, why hast thou forsaken me?" To be forsaken of God is hell.

2. *Jesus delivered us from hell.* That too was part of the curse upon sin, and awaits the sinner after death. "Depart from me" is the culmination of God's punishment. Jesus suffered that for us too. In our greatest temptations, in our struggle against all evil and the devil himself, this is our assurance and comfort, that Jesus has delivered us from hell.

Should one ask why are we not entirely free from temptations and the devil then now, since Jesus descended into hell? Because the old Adam must die and the new man in the struggle must be made strong. But the ship does not founder in the storm; the Pilot is on board and the harbor lights are penetrating the fog. In our struggle we do not perish, because Christ bore all that one could suffer in time and eternity, and he suffered these hellish agonies for us.

It would be interesting to quote Bible passages of those who differ from the Reformed view, but we know that all can be interpreted satisfactorily and in harmony with our viewpoint.

Without Christ, hell awaits. In Christ, salvation is complete. Without this article, eternal death is not dealt with. In our struggles, in life, in death, in the judgment day, our anchor holds, for *he descended into hell.*

1. Prove that this step of humiliation was not a historical continuation of the previous four steps.
2. If the summing up of the four steps of humiliation is intended, what benefit is this article to us?
3. Could we just omit this article?
4. Does "hell" mean the grave or the place of the damned?
5. Do the torments of hell, from which Christ delivers, await the sinner?
6. Does this article deal with Christ as God, or Christ as Mediator?
7. May we meditate on the mystery of the body and soul of Christ from Friday evening until the Resurrection? Ps. 16.
8. What do others believe about this article?
9. If this article is explained as a triumph should it not belong under the state of exaltation?

## He Lives

QUESTION 45 — *What does the resurrection of Christ profit us?*

ANSWER — First, by his resurrection he hath overcome death, that he might make us partakers of that righteousness which he had purchased for us by his death. Secondly, we are also by his power raised up a new life. And lastly, the resurrection of Christ is a sure pledge of our blessed resurrection.

●

Christ is risen! The resurrection heralds victory of Life over Death! The darkness of the curse is dispelled by the brilliant Sun of Righteousness of Easter morning. Christ conquered the powers of hell and death in his resurrection.

The Gospels teach the historical and circumstantial evidences of the resurrection. The Acts deal with the newly enthused disciples after the risen Saviour poured out the Holy Spirit. Paul places before us the inconceivable alternative: If Christ is not risen, all is in vain.

This tremendous subject is treated in our Catechism in one question and answer, while the ascension is dealt with in four questions. Our present-day observation of these two events is usually in the reverse ratio. One might defend this apparent contradiction by stating that the resurrection is — or should be — remembered *every* Lord's Day, but the theological reason is found in the historical background when the Catechism was written. No one denied the resurrection then, while the subject of the ascension was disputed in connection with Roman Catholic and Lutheran practices.

A century ago the liberal interpretation began against the Biblical teaching of Jesus' resurrection. First it was, as in the Gospel story, doubted, then denied. If the Catechism were written today, we would devote more space to the apologetic approach which was not needed then, inasmuch as all Christians believed that Christ rose from the dead. Today Biblical study and joyful witness must combine to accentuate our faith in the living Christ. That emphasis is fourfold:

1. *Christ has overcome death.* No Roman Catholic crucifix nor the ghostly Mexican display of a bloody cadaver constitute our true Biblical concept of Christ; we have a *living* Saviour! He conquered our last and most terrible enemy, death.

2. *We are partakers of that righteousness which he had purchased for us by his death.* Romans 4:25. This does not mean the imputed righteousness which comes to the believer by faith in his atonement and through the Holy Spirit. It means the state of righteousness before God which Christ gained through his resurrection, and which we share as members of his body.

3. *New life.* We are raised up to a *new* life. Was there an *old* life? Were we not spiritually dead? Yes, but that death was not the state of inactivity of a dead stone, but a process of constant decay of our efforts and opposition to God's will. Now we are reunited to God. In this new union new life comes, which instead of decay and opposition brings fruition and obedience to the divine will.

4. *A sure pledge of our* blessed *resurrection.* Again the adjective is important: there is a resurrection unto damnation also. No argument is intended here about life after death. That comes

in the discussion of "Resurrection of the body," but a pledge in Christ's resurrection that ours also will be a blessed resurrection.

When we have vague ideas concerning Christ's passion, we find little joy in Christ's resurrection. But when we are drawn by the redemptive power of the cross, we glory in the renewing power of the resurrection!

1. Name the five steps in the state of Exaltation.
2. What type of the resurrection is mentioned in the O. T.?
3. What did Jesus prophesy concerning his own resurrection?
4. What did the resurrection prove in regard to Christ and his redemptive work?
5. What do we call the 40 days before Easter?
6. How many appearances are mentioned of the risen Saviour?
7. Name the three-fold benefit for the believer.
8. When is Easter celebrated in the Church year?
9. What is the "power of his resurrection"?

# Received Up Into Glory

QUESTION 46 — *How dost thou understand these words, "He ascended into Heaven"?*

ANSWER — That Christ, in sight of his disciples, was taken up from earth into heaven: and that he continues there for our interest, until he comes again to judge the quick and the dead.

QUESTION 47 — *Is not Christ then with us, even to the end of the world, as he hath promised?*

ANSWER — Christ is very man and very God: with respect to his human nature, he is no more on earth; but with respect to his Godhead, majesty, grace, and Spirit, he is at no time absent from us.

●

After the glorious resurrection, when Jesus showed himself alive by many infallible proofs — witness the many appearances — from Mount Olivet he was received up into glory. I Tim. 3:16.

The large place in the Catechism devoted to this subject pleads for a renewed interest on the part of the believer in the ascended Lord. Observation of Ascension as a holy day is practically unknown in Protestant churches. In many Reformed

Churches this subject is referred to the Sunday before or after Ascension — if then.

Four questions are discussed in the 14th Lord's Day in regard to *where* Jesus is. Then follows another Lord's Day concerning *what* Jesus does.

Three points of emphasis merit our appreciation. Jesus is:

1. *In Heaven.* Prophesied by the Psalmists; typified by Enoch and Elijah; witnessed by the disciples; confirmed by the angels; preached by the Apostles — Jesus ascended *truly;* there is nothing figurative or symbolic about it. He also ascended *visibly,* not like our spirits return unto God at the hour of our death, but in sight of his disciples. Here we differ from the Lutherans, who maintain that at the Ascension Christ's body became omni-present, which excludes the statement of being in a definite place, which the angels referred to as heaven. This interpretation of the Ascension is in reality a nullification of our Confession.

And Jesus ascended *locally*: Mt. Olivet is explicitly mentioned to form the contrast with earth and heaven. Both are places. Heaven is a place. Heaven is not a condition, attitude or state of mind. God created heaven and earth. Earth is a place: heaven is a place too, concerning which the Bible tells us that it is created; that it is God's throne; that Jesus went to prepare us a place there and which John describes in soul-lifting concepts where language fails and imagination lags. Heaven is not a Beautiful Isle of Somewhere: Jesus came from heaven and ascended into heaven.

2. *Continuing in Heaven.* He is there for our interest; that three-fold interest is discussed in Question 49, and Jesus' activities in the following Lord's Day.

3. *Returning from Heaven* to judge the quick and the dead. This also has a separate consideration in the discussion of the article: "from whence he shall come." At least in two places Reformed doctrine definitely teaches the Second Advent, the charge of many who claim to have a monopoly on this subject notwithstanding.

Now the question becomes appropriate: Is not Christ with us, even as he hath promised? His human nature is no longer with us; we cannot break some alabaster box of precious ointment at his feet. His physical presence is not with us at Communion or in the Mass. Yet he is present: with respect to his Godhead, majesty, grace and Spirit he is at no time absent from us. This is an unforgettable statement. This is the sheet anchor of our faith in the Ascended Lord. It should be indelibly written upon our memory and engraved upon the tablets of the believing heart. In our joys and in our sorrows; in our work and in our worship; in life and death with his Godhead, majesty, grace and Spirit he is at no time absent from us.

When we are conscious of that presence and when we cultivate that presence, we will no longer consider Ascension the least of our Church observances.

1. How many days did Jesus remain on earth after his resurrection?
2. What did Jesus do in that period?
3. Why did he not remain with us?
4. Was the Ascension typified?
5. Was the Ascension prophesied?
6. Who witnessed the Ascension?
7. Was the Ascension a sign of divine approval upon Christ's work?
8. Until when does Christ remain in Heaven?
9. What are Christ's activities in Heaven?
10. In connection with the Ascension, what do we learn from Stephen's death and Saul's conversion?
11. Is Ascension Day of minor importance in the Church year?

## The Lost Chord

QUESTION 48 — *But if his human nature is not present wherever His Godhead is, are not then two natures in Christ separated from one another?*

ANSWER — Not at all, for since the Godhead is incomprehensible and omnipresent, it must necessarily follow, that the same is not limited with the human nature he assumed, and yet remains personally united to it.

QUESTION 49 — *Of what advantage to us is Christ's ascension into heaven?*

ANSWER — First, That he is our Advocate in the presence of his Father in heaven. Secondly, That we have our flesh in heaven as a sure pledge, that he, as the head, will also take up to himself, us his members. Thirdly, That he sends us his Spirit as an earnest, by whose power we "seek the things which are above, where Christ sitteth on the right hand of God, and not things on earth."

●

This is the Lost Chord in the Ascension Meditation. Even when Ascension is observed, this difficult question is readily ignored. Yet the Reformed view here expounded is most essential in contending for our faith. In Question 18 we learned of the two natures of Christ *In One Person,* which can be distinguished but may not be separated. Now in the Ascension, are not these two natures separated from one another?

Being delivered from the error of Christ's physical presence, by upholding that he is still with us with respect to his Godhead, majesty, grace and Spirit, can we maintain that these two natures still are one and undivided?

A similar difficulty was discussed in Question 41, and the Belgic Confession 19 was quoted. What did not happen at Christ's burial could not happen at the Ascension. In his Ascension he contributed immortality to His human nature, but his true human nature is not lost nor separated from his divine nature.

An easy way out would be to say like the Lutherans that his human nature became more and more divine: the divine nature permeated the human nature till it found its culmination during the Ascension.

But then the Ascension is no longer real and true, for then his body receives the divine attribute of omnipresence: how could it ascend into heaven? Yet, in ascribing deity to his humanity, there appears a plausibility for the Roman Catholic and Lutheran errors of trans- and con-substantiation.

However, this is a gross misconception. Human nature is created by God, and as such is a creature, and not the Creator. Human nature cannot attain unto deity, even in the Ascension; human nature can never be God. To be God — that was the devil's temptation and downfall in heaven, for what more could he want in heaven? To be God — that was the devil's instigation to Adam's temptation — what else did he lack in Paradise? Now shall we make the same salute to the devil again? No created being becomes the Creator. God keeps that for himself. Does Christ's humanity become permeated by the deity culminating during the Ascension? The answer is, No.

Are these two natures separated then? Not at all, for since the Godhead is incomprehensible and omnipresent, it must necessarily follow that the same is not limited with the human nature he assumed, and remains personally united with it. So do we think of our soul and body as one. Yet our body may be in the Church and our soul can be at home, or vice versa. But they remain one, even though the soul can be where the body cannot go; they are not separated even though they function in different places. Now in Christ's human nature he cannot come to our aid, but the divine nature can and does; his Godhead is omnipresent, that is for our never-ending comfort.

That Christ is in heaven means to the believer that he is our Advocate in the presence of his Father in heaven; that he is our Pledge of heaven, inasmuch as he is the Head and will take unto himself his members; he is our Earnest of the Spirit who directs our hearts to the things which are above.

Christ's Ascension demands more than the believer's casual attention. Instead of the Lost Chord the Ascension merits an Ecclesiastical Symphony!

1. Where is Christ's human nature now?
2. In which four-fold capacity is he at no time absent from us?
3. Is there, then, a separation between the two natures of Christ?
4. Who teach that Christ's body received the divine attribute of omnipresence at the Ascension?
5. If Christ ascended into Heaven, can we ever hold the "real," that is, "physical presence," in the Sacrament of Communion?
6. How are we comforted by his presence?
7. What three advantages are here taught in Christ's ascension?
8. What commandment did Jesus give before his Ascension?

# King of Kings and Lord of Lords

QUESTION 50 — *Why is it added, "And sitteth at the right hand of God"?*

ANSWER — Because Christ is ascended into heaven for this end, that he might there appear as head of his Church, by whom the Father governs all things.

QUESTION 51 — *What profit is this glory of Christ our head unto us?*

ANSWER — First, That by his Holy Spirit, he poureth out heavenly graces upon us his members; and then that by his power he defends and preserves us against all enemies.

※

Christ, the Head of the Church! No secondary consideration is to be given to this article of our faith. Some do this by ignoring it altogether, or mistakenly think that the Ascension and the sitting at the right hand of God are virtually the same in their intent. Far from being the backwash of the Ascension, we find ourselves in the full current of the main stream of Christ's Exaltation, the place of honor and power. Here we meet the error of Roman Catholicism as regards Christ's Headship, and Scofield's unscriptural abeyance theory denying Christ's Kingship. Here we hail Christ (I Peter 3:22), angels and authorities and powers being made subject unto him.

Thirteen times the Bible describes Jesus as *sitting* at the right hand of God; twice as *being* and once as *standing* there, when he received the spirit of Stephen the martyr. This third step in the Exaltation is to be considered in relation:

1. *To Christ.* Could Christ receive honor, when it is impossible to add dignity to the deity? Not in his capacity as second person of the Trinity, but inasmuch as he emptied himself of his glory in his Incarnation, he is restored in the Exaltation. This he receives: All power is *given* unto me (Eph. 1:20). God *set* him at his own right hand.

2. *To the Trinity.* Did God abdicate his throne or abrogate his power? This article itself rescues us from any such misconception, when it states: God the Father Almighty, and also refers to the Spirit in the explanation. It is the Trinity through which Christ executes the divine plan and power.

3. *To the Church.* Christ is the Head of the Church (Eph. 1:22), and as such pours out his blessings, defends, intercedes — Belgic Confession 26 — and governs all things. *Head* means both Organic Union and Authority: Col. 1:13. Some "heads" have organic union and not authority, like a head of a family. Some "heads" have authority and no organic union, like the head of a business. Christ has both. In the mystical union with our legal and spiritual Head, the believer's Justification finds its sure foundation. Now we learn to grasp the importance of Christ at the right hand of God as Head of the Church!

But then the Pope cannot be the Head of the Church, as Luther stated, for then the Church would be a monstrosity, having two heads! Christ has not abdicated his authority. Nor can the Pope be the Vicar of Christ, for Christ is neither absent nor is he incapacitated: he is with us, and all power is given unto him!

And we must also warn against those who deny Christ's Kingship, like some Protestants do: Acts 2:36. "God has made that same Jesus both *Lord* and Christ." No, his kingship is not deferred till his kingdom is complete! He is King now. Why say "head" then? Because the Bible calls Jesus "Head of the

Church." And because "Head" still expresses Organic Union and Authority, while the word "King" is subject to change: we have a president as head of our nation.

So we cling to Peter's statement, Acts 2:36, and Paul's affirmation, Col. 1:18, that in all things he might have the preeminence. And we remember the favorite name for our Saviour: Our *Lord* Jesus Christ. And once and again we are thrilled when our souls are lifted in the oratorio, joining John's acclaim: King of Kings, and Lord of Lords!

1. Why is this article important?
2. What errors do we here oppose?
3. What is the meaning of sitting, standing, or being at the right hand of God?
4. What does this statement mean for the Church?
5. Discuss its relation to Christ and to the Trinity.
6. Discuss organic union and authority in Christ as Head of the Church.
7. Why do we not say King, but Head of the Church?
8. How does Christ as King preserve and defend us?

## That Blessed Hope

QUESTION 52 — *What comfort is it to thee that "Christ shall come again to judge the quick and the dead"?*

ANSWER — That in all my sorrows and persecutions, with uplifted head, I look for the very same person, who before offered himself for my sake, to the tribunal of God, and hath removed all curse from me, to come as judge from heaven: who shall cast all his and my enemies into everlasting condemnation, but shall translate me, with all his chosen ones, to himself into heavenly joys and glory.

●

Though stirred by the premillennial emphasis of our day, we will overcome the temptation to depart from this ancient advent explanation, and to enter the controversy of *Pre-, Post-,* and *A-.* It is altogether regrettable, that this comforting doctrine is used as a sword to slay brethren who are like-minded regarding their faith in the coming of our Lord, but are differently-minded regarding the details of "that blessed hope." Here it is placed in the light of Christian comfort. And that applies to our Reformed Church. Others may enter this arena as a theological battleground, but our three Forms of Unity — the Heidelberg Catechism, the Five Canons and the 37 Articles — do not furnish us with a blueprint of God's plan for eternity. Hence there is considerable liberty of diversity among our members, many of whom moderately but literally love to speak of the Thousand Years, the Golden Age and the Jews' Return. As long as they do not draw unbiblical conclusions, these views are permitted in our Church, for they are extra-confessional.

Adhering then to this ancient Faith of our Fathers, here we learn that Jesus' coming again is:

1. *Personal and Visible.* "I look for the very same person," Acts 3:21. Belgic Confession 37. Visible: every eye shall see him. With our radio and TV, science confirms that possibility, but God revealed it long before science used God's laws to build up our feeble faith.

2. *Comforting and Sustaining.* In our sorrows and persecutions, with uplifted head, we have a hope that maketh not ashamed, but comforts us in defeat and sustains us in discouragements; evil will not always endure. Satan will not have power over us.

3. *Unexpected and Sudden.* Some may scorn and scoff: where is the promise of his coming? II Peter 3:4. Ignorance may be blind in spite of the signs that precede: the Antichrist overthrown; the Gospel preached; the Jews to return to their Messiah; the Falling Away, but he will come as a thief in the night.

4. *Glorious and Triumphant.* In all the glory of his majesty will he come as judge from heaven. Not like the Babe of Bethlehem nor like the Man of Sorrows will he appear. The sign of the Son of Man will be seen. The dead in Christ will be raised. All must appear before his judgment seat: one Advent, one resurrection unto everlasting damnation and his own into heavenly joys and glory; one judgment day. Heaven and earth will acknowledge him. Every knee shall bow before him. There will be a restitution of all things in the new heaven and new earth, wherein righteousness dwelleth.

This is "that blessed hope" of all those who love his appearing. Human speculation can add neither to Christ's glory nor to the believer's comfort. And when we cannot fit the various pieces into one complete logical and theological pattern, let us be satisfied to believe that the revealed things are for us and for our

children. And let us with uplifted head look for the very same
Jesus who died for our sin. And let us devoutly join John in his
closing prayer: Even so, come, Lord Jesus!

1. Is the return of Christ promised and predicted?
2. In what capacity shall Christ return?
3. Are his chosen people then translated?
4. What is the order of the resurrection?
5. What is the time of Christ's return?
6. What signs precede his coming?
7. What signs accompany his coming?
8. How is Christ's promised return related to our Christian interest
   and activity?
9. Do we hopefully look for his return?
10. Discuss Millennium; Advent-Parousia; Man of Sin; Antichrist; Son
    of Perdition; Apostasy.

## The Holy Spirit

QUESTION 53 — *What dost thou believe concerning the Holy
Ghost?*

ANSWER — First, that he is true and co-eternal God with the
Father and the Son; secondly, that he is also given me, to
make me, by a true faith, partaker of Christ and all his benefits, that he may comfort me and abide with me forever.

●

Resting squarely on Biblical grounds, two hundred statements
could be made concerning the Holy Spirit in addition to the two
here given. This abbreviated treatment is all the more disappointing since it follows the detailed description of our Saviour.
There we marveled at his conception, knelt by his cradle; stood
by his cross. We listened to the angels and traveled with the
Wise Men and wept with the daughters of Jerusalem. And every
minute detail had a particular blessing for the believer. But when
the Holy Spirit is considered there is such a dire poverty of
teaching and reflection.

From the Modernist, who explains the Holy Spirit as impulses
for righteousness which come to men; and from the heretical sects
who totally ignore the Holy Spirit, we could expect this. But
the Christian! Be it known to him that he travels dangerously
near the abyss of self-righteousness who at any one moment of
his journey travels alone, without the Holy Spirit. Who speaks
of the gift and the gifts of the Spirit? Who dares to proclaim
as did Paul: "It seemed good unto the Holy Spirit and unto us"?

Who honors the Holy Spirit as Intercessor, quickener, witness, comforter, paraclete, revealer, solicitor, teacher, guide? Who is concerned about vexing, grieving, resisting the Holy Spirit; the sin against the Holy Spirit? We pray to God the Father — God the Son, but what part does the Holy Spirit have in our prayers? Facing all these activities, these two essentials of our faith in the Holy Spirit are pre-eminent:

1. *The Holy Spirit's relation to God the Father and God the Son.* He is true and co-essential God with the Father and the Son. The Holy Spirit is God. The Holy Spirit is a person. He has divine names, attributes, works and honor. He proceeds from the Father and the Son. He is the third person in the Trinity.

These Biblical facts we learned in Question 25. Here we confess them as our personal faith in the Holy Spirit.

2. *The Holy Spirit's relation to the believer.*

That relation is expressed in four distinct and important phrases:

(a) *"that he is also given me."* "Have ye received the Holy Ghost?" was the question to the early disciples. At Jesus' prayer, he is given (John 14:16). Our Heavenly Father will give him to us when we ask (Luke 11:13). We must ask for him. He is not bought as Simon thought (Acts 8:18). That he is given to us is all important, when the consciousness of our need of Christ brings us to new life in regeneration.

(b) *"to make me a partaker of Christ and all his benefits."* The believer is part of the body, of which Christ is the head. With Christ we receive all benefits when the Holy Spirit leads us into all truth. Many of these truths and benefits are with us in heir-incipient stages. Now the Spirit encourages us to come to a full fruition. True faith is necessary. The Word and the Sacraments are the means used by the Spirit.

(c) *"that he may comfort me."* Jesus calls him "another comforter." Christ is the great Consoler in sorrow. The Spirit does not comfort us because of the physical absence of Christ, as some think. But through his indwelling he keeps the spark of faith alive in our soul, comforting us in our struggle against our own evil spirit and against the spirit of Satan, enabling us to grow in our Christian consecration and to fight the good fight of faith.

(d) *"and abide with me forever."* That is the Lord's promise in John 14:16, and that is our sheet anchor in our soul's distress.

When the Spirit is with us, he remains with us (Psalm 138:8 — John 10:28).

1. Prove by his names and attributes that the Holy Spirit is God.
2. Prove by his works and honors that the Holy Spirit is God.
3. Mention Biblical names of the Holy Spirit.
4. How does the Spirit convict us of sin?
5. How does the Holy Spirit intercede **in** us and **for** us?
6. What is the work of the Holy Spirit as Comforter?
7. Mention gifts of the Spirit. I Cor. 12.
8. Mention the fruit of the Spirit. Gal. 5:22
9. Name sins against the Holy Spirit.
10. Why is the Holy Spirit called Holy?

## The Holy Catholic Church

QUESTION 54 — *What believest thou concerning the "Holy Catholic Church" of Christ?*

ANSWER — That the Son of God from the beginning to the end of the world, gathers, defends, and preserves to himself, by his Spirit and Word, out of the whole human race, a Church chosen to everlasting life, agreeing in true faith, and that I am, and forever shall remain, a living member thereof.

●

Undoubtedly, when the word *Church* is mentioned, our minds picture to us some place of worship dear to our hearts. To it, whether built of sods as in pioneer days, or constructed like a dream in stone, our childhood feet were led. There the sign of the covenant was placed upon our brow. There we received religious instruction and made confession of our faith in Christ. There the vows of marriage were publicly given, and it was in that place too where comfort was received when we mourned our dead. That place of weekly worship was the home of our soul; the altar of our devotion; the communion of the saints.

However, much as we appreciate our places of worship, whenever the New Testament speaks of the Church, not buildings, but believers, are designated. The Hebrews gloried in Solomon's temple, and, after the exile, the temple was their chief concern. But Jesus spoke of people when he said: "I will build my church," and thus prepared us for Heaven where John in his vision saw no temple therein (Rev. 21:22). Believers are called the building of Christ, and concerning them we learn that they are:

1. *Chosen* to everlasting life; chosen from the beginning to the end of the world; chosen out of the whole human race.

—75—

"Ye have not chosen me, but I have chosen you." "I have chosen you out of the world" (John 15:16 and 19). So writes Paul: "According as he has chosen us in him, before the foundation of the world" (Eph. 1:4) They are not chosen because of their nobility, nor because of their fore-seen faith or good works, but because of the Sovereign grace of the triune God (Rom. 8:29). This Bible truth places the church head and shoulders above every organization in the whole world because of its divine origin.

*2. Gathered, Defended, and Preserved.* All three persons of the Trinity have their part, but as the Church of Christ, he gathers them that are chosen by his Word and Spirit. It is Christ who became like unto us, sin excepted, to redeem his own, and gave himself as a willing sacrifice; who defends his Church, so that the gates of hell cannot prevail against it; who preserves the Church, so that when we confess *one, Holy, Catholic* Church, its *unity, sanctity and universality is maintained.* That Church agrees in true faith. Looking at various denominations, one may shake his head, but it is true of the invisible Church. Its *unity* is in its faith in one head, Christ (Eph. 4:5).

When the invisible Church reveals itself in a visible way through organizations, government, Sacraments, witnessing, etc., that visible Church is then no longer perfect. It is in the process of perfection when both the invisible Church and the visible Church shall be one in glory.

*3. Kept.* As an article of our faith, a personal confession of faith is expressed: "that I am, and forever shall remain a living member thereof." That we are thus kept is possible also only by the power of God.

This article reads: "I believe *in* a holy catholic church." Neither in the original nor in the question is that word *in* found. I do not believe *in* the Church as I believe in God. I believe in Christ, and where Christ is, there is the Church.

1. Do we speak of buildings or believers when the Church is referred to in the Bible?
2. What is the Church militant and triumphant?
3. What is the visible and invisible Church?
4. What three attributes does the Creed mention?
5. What is the Unity and what is the Union of the Church?
6. What are the three evidences of the true Church?
7. What is the discipline of the Church?
8. What is the Liturgy of the Church?
9. What is the Constitution of the Church?
10. What are the three Forms of Unity?

# The Communion of Saints

QUESTION 55 — *What do you understand by "The Communion of saints"?*

ANSWER — First, that all and every one who believes, being members of Christ, are in common, partakers of him, and of all his riches and gifts; Secondly, that every one must know it to be his duty, readily and cheerfully to employ his gifts, for the advantage and salvation of other members.

●

"Behold, how good and how pleasant it is for brethren to dwell together in unity" (Ps. 133:1). This part of our confession furnishes much food for thought when we learn that this is the only addition to the article pertaining to the Church. Not the Church and her government, world-wide task, or a hundred other issues that press to the foreground when we mention the church, but the one outstanding consideration is: the communion of the saints. That, and that alone keeps the church in its onward march, when it practices:

1. *Communion with Christ.* That is the secret of the continued success of the church. When believers are the body of Christ, it is of supreme importance to maintain living contact with the Head, Christ. Jesus emphasizes this again and again in symbolic figures when he speaks of the Vine and the Branches; one Flock and one Shepherd; Shepherd and Sheep. The Lord's Supper is rightly called Communion. In that union the believer is a partaker of Christ and of all his riches and gifts. Break that union and, like wires that have been cut, we lose our light and our very life.

2. *Communion with other members.* Of the early church it was said, "Behold, how they love one another." Strange but true, that is not always evident in our dealing with our fellow members. The strongest tie that binds ought to be the tie of our common faith. Worldly organizations would not be so flourishing, if Christian people "knew it to be their duty, readily and cheerfully, to employ their gifts for the advantage of other members." "And for the salvation of other members." "Advantage" may have reference to daily and social needs, but "salvation" applies to our spiritual life. While it is true that we cannot give salvation to others, gifts for salvation are mentioned: to bear the infirmities of the weak; to cultivate the spirit of peace; to consider others higher than one's self.

Think also of "other members" outside of our own little Zion. Our spiritual horizon must not be limited by our myopic vision. When we are ecumenically minded, let us not sacrifice truth for the sake of uniformity. Remember there are many members in the body of Christ and there is a diversity of operations (I Cor. 12). In our union with Christ lies the unity of the believers. Our States have different laws, but we have one Federal Constitution. The rainbow displays a variety of hues. One note played on four pianos is not ideal harmony.

But we are in sore need of co-operation with and recognition of others: in our mission efforts, in religious publications; in education, in transfer of membership, in matters of discipline, in community moral issues; in mutual defense against the common foe; in attending and belonging to "other" denominations when our own is not represented; in welcoming at the Lord's table other believers where true Communion and Union is symbolized, realized and practiced.

"The fellowship of kindred minds is like to that above" and it flourishes into full bloom when we practice our confession concerning "The communion of saints."

1. What is communion with Christ?
2. Where is this practiced?
3. What do we mean by Communion with fellow-believers?
4. In what spheres of Christian life is that practiced?
5. What sin makes communion with fellow-believers difficult?
6. Mention spheres of possible co-operation with others.
7. Are all denominational divisions wrong?
8. What is ecumenicity?
9. What should be the test for all proposed Church unions?

## The Forgiveness of Sins

QUESTION 56 — *What believest thou concerning "the forgiveness of sins"?*

ANSWER — That God, for the sake of Christ's satisfaction, will no more remember my sins, neither my corrupt nature, against which I have to struggle all my life long; but will graciously impute to me the righteousness of Christ, that I may never be condemned before the tribunal of God.

●

Of the three gifts to the Church, forgiveness of sins is the first. That is the very core of Christianity that brings the comforting joy and peace which comes to the pardoned soul. Not a shout of triumph is heard, but an amazingly quiet confidence comes when we rightfully believe and appreciate that God for Christ's sake hath forgiven us.

And why is that a gift to the Church? It surely does not mean that the Church forgives, or that having been forgiven we now can belong to the Church. No, when we belong to the Church, our sins are forgiven. In connection with our confession concerning the church, we learned that its essential part is the communion of saints. In our union with Christ forgiveness is received. It is the joyful task of the Church through preaching and Baptism and the Lord's Supper to bring the good news that "the blood of Jesus Christ his Son cleanseth us from all sin" (I John 1:7).

The Psalmist glories in the fact that "with thee is forgiveness" and refers to the "tribunal of God," indicating God's righteousness which requires punishment. Yet the Old Testament shows the way to God's forgiveness, when it speaks of sacrifices for sin, its being blotted out and covered over (Ps. 32). All these fore-shadowed the sacrifice of the Lamb of God, "in whom we have redemption, even forgiveness of sin." In the New Testament we are plainly taught that our forgiveness depends on *Christ,* the blood supplied; *Water,* the blood applied; and the *Word* taught, all three describing different phases of the same transaction, and all mentioned in connection with forgiveness. First, the blood of Christ. God does not wipe the slate, nor send universal pardon, but "for the sake of Christ's satisfaction will no more remember my sins." God does not forgive without right or reason: Christ satisfied by his precious life, giving himself, his blood as the Lamb of God in our place. The *water* refers to the Holy Spirit: "Then will I sprinkle clean water upon you, and thou shalt be clean." "Rise and be baptized, that thy sins may be washed away." Baptism signifies the washing away of sin. The *Word* is the method of divine communication: "Now ye are clean through the word." Through the Word we learn of the need of repentance and confession. Like Bunyan's Christian we oft go through the mire of Doubt before we come to the door of Repentance. On that door is written *"knock"* and when the door opens it leads to the cross where the burden of our sin is rolled away.

Nor is there a contradiction when I learn that I have to struggle against my corrupt nature all my life long. The chapter on forgiveness is the opening chapter in the Christian life, and there are many more pages before the book is finished: our corrupt nature is not taken away until we cross the river of death. Various temptations come to us, now more than ever before. Yes, we are free from the *penalty* of sin, but we are not free from the *presence* of sin, nor are we free from the *power* of sin. Day by day we are in need of forgiveness, and power to overcome evil.

Now we know that it is not easy for God to forgive for he is holy, faithful and just. It was difficult, for God hates sin; it was possible, for he loves the sinner. Thus we stand before the divine tribunal never to be condemned because of Christ in whom "mercy and truth are met together; righteousness and peace have kissed each other" (Ps. 85:10).

The unrepented sin and the unconfessed sin is the unforgiven sin. That requires faith on our part; faith to believe, faith to confess, faith to forsake and to fight evil without and within. That we do only in our communion with Christ. And in that unity is the imputation of Christ's righteousness and the forgiveness of our sin.

1. What are the three gifts to the Church?
2. What is the way to forgiveness in the Old Testament?
3. What is required for forgiveness?
4. Who forgives sin?
5. How did Jesus secure our forgiveness?
6. What is the place of the blood, the water and the Word in forgiveness?
7. Does repentance mean penance?
8. Is the presence of sin and the power of sin still with us?
9. Was it easy for God to forgive sin?
10. What is the unpardonable sin?

## Resurrection of the Body and Life Everlasting

QUESTION 57 — *What comfort doth the resurrection of the body afford thee?*

ANSWER — That not only my soul, after this life, shall be immediately taken up to Christ its head; but also, that this my body, being raised by the power of Christ, shall be re-united with my soul, and made like unto the glorious body of Christ.

QUESTION 58 — *What comfort takest thou from the article of "life everlasting"?*

ANSWER — That since I now feel in my heart the beginning of eternal joy, after this life, I shall inherit perfect salvation, which "Eye hath not seen, nor ear heard, neither hath it entered into the heart of man to conceive," and that to praise God therein for ever!

●

Sin brought the curse of God on both body and soul. "In the sweat of thy brow shalt thou eat bread." Thorns and thistles on the soil, death for the body, are the physical results. Sin separated the soul from God.

Jesus suffered both in body and soul, so that as our perfect Saviour he enables body and soul to share his salvation. Hence we believe in the resurrection of the body and life everlasting when we claim the Saviour's: —

1. *Promise for the body.* This is not to be confused with life in the hereafter. Even the Indians believed in a happy hunting ground. But the body, shall it live again? "For there is hope of a tree, if it be cut down, that it will sprout again" (Job 14:7). Jesus uncompromisingly said, "All that are in the graves shall hear his voice," (John 5:28-29) and comfortingly promised, "Because I live, ye shall live also" (John 14:19). Then he crowned his words with his own resurrection, which makes Christianity unique in its resurrected Saviour and in its teaching of the resurrection of the body.

We may sing with the poet of the awakening Spring; we may look at analogies in nature like the butterfly from the chrysalis and the lily from the bulb, but our faith in this part of our Confession is: Christ arose. Paul poses the alternative in I Cor. 15, and staked his life and ministry on the hope of the resurrection. This mortal must put on immortality, but our bodies shall live whether they have been buried, burned or blown to pieces; God's Word does not fail.

2. *Promises for the soul.* What is the state of the soul after death? It shall be immediately taken up to Christ, its head.

No, our beloved dead are not in the grave, they are with the Lord. Tombstones often incorrectly state: *Here lies* . . . For that reason our stern forefathers frowned on decoration of the grave, funeral sermons and visits to the grave. We now think they were too severe. Christian people may comfort one another with prayer, song, and Scripture meditation. But we lift up our eyes unto Heaven where Jesus is, and where our loved ones are too.

No soul-sleep is taught. The soul is from God and cannot sleep whether in the body or when that body sleeps, for God spoke to men in their dreams. No Purgatory is taught, for the blood of Christ cleanses from all sin; and Paul asserts, "for to me to die is gain." Neither soul-sleep nor Purgatory would be gain. In death the spirit shall return to God who gave it (Ecc. 12:7).

3. *Promises for reunion* in life eternal. Question 57 teaches a reunion with our soul, when we shall be made like unto the glorious body of Christ. Daniel speaks of two resurrections, and Jesus says, in John 5:29, "And they shall come forth, they that have done good unto the resurrection of life; and they that have done evil unto the resurrection of damnation." For the ungodly it will be eternal death. For the saved, eternal life. That eternal life begins here, as the answer in Question 58 states: "I now feel in my heart the beginning of eternal joy; after this life I shall inherit perfect salvation." The book of Revelation in chapters 21 and 22 describes for us these perfections.

Life everlasting means a reunion of soul and body, a reunion with our loved ones in eternal bliss; and, best of all, there we will see Jesus.

1. Distinguish resurrection of the body from immortality.
2. What happens at the moment of death? Ec. 12:7
3. Is death separation or annihilation?
4. Is death a sleep?
5. What do Roman Catholics believe about Purgatory?
6. Is there a second chance after death?
7. What is the order of the resurrection? I Thess. 4:13
8. What does Jesus teach in John 5:28?
9. What kind of body will there be? I Cor. 15:50

# Justification by Faith

QUESTION 59 — *But what does it profit thee now that thou believest all this?*

ANSWER — That I am righteous in Christ before God, and an heir of eternal life.

QUESTION 60 — *How art thou righteous before God?*

ANSWER — Only by a true faith in Jesus Christ: so that, though my conscience accuse me that I have grossly transgressed all the commands of God and kept none of them, and am still inclined to all evil; notwithstanding, God, without any merit of mine, but only of mere grace, grants and imputes to me, the perfect satisfaction, righteousness and holiness of Christ; even so as if I never had had, nor committed any sin: yea, as if I had fully accomplished all that obedience which Christ hath accomplished for me; inasmuch as I embrace such benefit with a believing heart. ,

●

Though neither inspiration nor perfection is claimed for any part of the Catechism, yet as certain hymns or parts of our Liturgy become our prized possession, so this answer and the first are spiritual jewels. Both are like the dew of Hermon for a thirsty soul. The first answer of the Catechism reaches the depths of Christian experience in the comfort that we are the Lord's. The 60th answer raises the soul to the heights of faith in the joy as to *how* we are the Lord's.

How shall a man be just before God? was the perplexing question of Job 3500 years ago. In the middle ages this was the dispute resulting in the Reformation. Justification by faith or justification by works was the dividing wedge deeply driven into the heart of the Church. However, we are not left in the dark in this controversy when we are guided by the Word of God. "Being justified by faith, we have peace with God through our Lord Jesus Christ" (Rom. 5:1).

What is the Biblical conception of justification by faith?

We are plainly taught in God's Word that sinful man cannot fulfill the law, so that "the whole world is guilty before God" (Rom. 3:19), subject to his condemnation. Now when God condemns us, that does not make us guilty: we *are* guilty. And if God does not condemn us, that does not make us innocent. The act of declaring us innocent is called justification. Justification is a judicial act of God whereby in his infinite grace, based on the merits of Christ, the sinner is pronounced just.

But is not God just? Yes, and he is the justifier of the unjust. Something must have happened so that God could declare the sinner just. And that happened when Christ fulfilled the law for us by his perfect righteousness. "The chastisement of our peace was upon him; and with his stripes we are healed" (Isa. 53:5). When God sees us in Christ, imputing his righteousness unto us, it is as if "I had fully accomplished all the obedience which Christ has fulfilled for me." Now God grants and imputes unto us the perfect satisfaction, righteousness and holiness of Christ when we embrace such benefit with a believing heart.

So it was with Abraham who "believed God, and it was counted unto him for righteousness" (Rom. 4:3). As with Abraham, so with us. When God grants us that in his grace, there is only one way in which we can receive it, namely by our faith. Believing all this — i.e., the preceding Apostles' Creed — God's righteousness is received by faith in Christ. That faith looks away from self, our merits, our good works, and depends for time and eternity on the saving merits of our Lord Jesus Christ. If we do not trust in Christ and his redeeming blood, it does not profit us.

But when righteousness is imputed, is our sin still in the book? Is that imputation given with reservation? Does our conscience still reproach us?

Listen to this glorious truth: It is "as if I never had had, nor committed any sin." More we could not expect. Yet that imputation goes further still: Yea, as if I "had myself accomplished all the obedience which Christ hath accomplished for me." That is beyond all expectation and beyond all human imagination. But that is God's grace, his marvelous, infinite grace which is freely mine, inasmuch as I embrace Christ's benefits with a believing heart. So wonderful, so divine is justification by faith!

1. What is Justification by faith?
2. What is imputation?
3. Who teach Justification by good works?
4. What is the place of grace and faith in Justification?
5. Does faith follow or precede Justification?
6. What is the place of good works in Justification?
7. Is Justification an inward act?
8. What is the ground for Justification?
9. Can we be assured of Justification?
10. How far does Justification go?

# Justification and Faith

QUESTION 61 — *Why sayest thou, that thou art righteous by faith only?*

ANSWER — Not that I am acceptable to God, on account of the worthiness of my faith, but because only the satisfaction, righteousness and holiness of Christ is my righteousness before God, and that I cannot receive and apply the same to myself in any other way, than by faith only.

●

Justification deals with God who justifies, and the believer who is justified. From God's standpoint that transaction calls for grace; from our standpoint it demands faith. Hence we can speak of justification by grace and by faith. Why, then, do you say that you are righteous by faith only? asks the catechism. Surely not because we overlook or minimize grace, but because we want to be positive about that faith. God's grace is without question of sincerity and verity. But our faith? Does it play a part, however small, in justification? Is it a contributing factor in justification? There is need of that faith, but what is the place and the value of it?

Now we say that we are righteous by faith only, because we maintain:

1. *The unworthiness* of that faith. Not that faith is useless, or needless, or worthless. We cannot even please God without faith. But in the consideration of justification we cannot say that faith is the distinction between the believer and the unbeliever, and that therefore God justifies him. That is not so for in justification the child of God appears ungodly. Otherwise he is not in need of justification. See the first part of the answer in Question 60. Hence I am not acceptable to God on account of the worthiness of my faith.

And when we are justified, such is the sinful inclination of the human heart, and such are Satan's soul-destroying seductions, that the believer might look upon his faith as part of his justification. But did not the Holy Spirit awaken that faith in us? Did not the Holy Spirit strengthen that faith in us? Are we now by incipient stages to credit ourselves for our justification, even in a small part? No, that last vestige must be eradicated; the last fort must be surrendered. None of self and all of thee, is a lesson we do not learn overnight; but with the help of the Holy Spirit, there we must stand.

2. *The perfection* of Christ's merit for that faith. As in Question 60, so here that merit of Christ is threefold and complete. There is satisfaction: Christ paid for our sin; righteousness: Christ recognized God in his right to punish sin; and holiness: Christ fulfilled the law which was broken by sin. Now what can be added to that? What needs to be added to that? Absolutely nothing!

3. *The application* of that righteousness by faith. I cannot receive it in any other way. That's why we say that we are justified by faith! Faith is not causal but instrumental. Faith is like the hand of the beggar who cannot credit his hand for the generosity of the giver, but without holding out his hand he cannot receive. So the important issue is not: How strong is your faith? but: How able is Christ? And our faith receives Christ's satisfaction, righteousness and holiness. That gives all the glory to God; all the honor to Christ; and all the benefit to us.

We must not confuse justification and regeneration. Justification is God's work outside of us; regeneration is God's work within us.

And we must distinguish justification from sanctification; justification is one finished act of God; sanctification is a process of a life time.

Justification is like a fountain of living water given us instead of the poisonous stream of our own righteousness. It is the pillar of our faith. It is the sword against the ungodly and the antichrist. In life and death it is the believer's joy that he has peace with God through our Lord Jesus Christ. Thus, truly, "we are the Lord's."

1. What two sides in justification are to be considered?
2. Is God's grace subject to doubt?
3. Are we acceptable to God on account of the worthiness of our faith?
4. What is the three-fold perfection of Christ's merit?
5. Explain that faith is not causal but instrumental.
6. Can we receive the merit of Christ in any other way than by faith?
7. Distinguish justification and regeneration.
8. Distinguish justification and sanctification.

# Justification and Good Works

QUESTION 62 — *But why can not our good works be the whole or part of our righteousness before God?*

ANSWER — Because that the righteousness, which can be approved of before the tribunal of God, must be absolutely perfect, and in all respects conformable to the divine law: and also that our best works in this life are all imperfect and defiled with sin.

QUESTION 63 — *What! do not our good works merit, which yet God will reward in this and in a future life?*

ANSWER — This reward is not of merit, but of grace.

QUESTION 64 — *But does not this doctrine make men careless and profane?*

ANSWER — By no means: for it is impossible that those, who are implanted into Christ by a true faith, should not bring forth fruits of thankfulness.

●

Having learned that justification by faith and good works no more mix than oil and water, we might conclude that the whole subject of good works is hereby dismissed. This is by no means the case. Later on, in connection with the commandments, we again deal with good works; there is the discussion of sanctification and good works. Here the discussion is justification and good works.

Three questions are posited:

1. *Are good works part of our righteousness before God?*

For the Christian, faith demands good works. Early in life we learned that prayer is the chief good work. Almsgiving, sacrifices of praise, and thanksgiving are mentioned as acceptable unto God. Jesus emphasized them. Think of the Beatitudes. And read Matt. 5:16 and Matt. 6:4. Paul maintains that we are "created in Christ Jesus unto good works, which God hath before ordained that we should walk in them" (Eph. 2:9). And James' teaching is well-known (Jas. 2:17).

But are they all or part of justification? Roman Catholicism answers in the affirmative. It claims that Jesus paid for our eternal punishment, but we must pay for our temporal sins now and later in Purgatory. Money may be paid to pray the departed soul out of this latter place of torment. The Bible opposes all this most strongly. The best of our good works are still sinful and cannot be part of our righteousness before God. And they need not be, for we have a perfect Saviour. Making that claim is "to bring Christ down from above" (Rom. 10:6).

2. *Do not our good works merit reward here and hereafter?*

Certainly, but this reward is not of merit, but of grace. We do not merit Heaven thereby. Again, this is in opposition to the Roman Catholic teaching. They hold that good works are credited toward eternal life. Some are even declared to have more than needed, works of supererogation, so that saints can help others of their abundant supply. This heresy is again derogatory to the perfect and sufficient sacrifice of Christ. Yes, there will be rewards, but they are not merit, not wages, but rewards of grace.

3. *Does not this teaching make men careless and profane?*

Paul seemed to have these people in mind when he wrote, "Shall we continue in sin, that grace may abound?" But his answer was, "God forbid, how shall we, that are dead to sin, live any longer therein" (Rom. 6:12)? Antinomians of later days also held that inasmuch as their sins were forgiven they were under no restraint of divine law any longer. They were careless and profane, and showed by their ungodly fruits that they were not implanted into Christ. For if Christ is the vine and we are the branches, then it is impossible that we should not bring forth fruits of thankfulness. The tree is known by its fruit. Being one with Christ we will do our utmost with the help of the Holy Spirit and the Word of God to guard against all sins.

To depend on our good works wholly or in part for our salvation is robbing Christ and his atonement of his honor as our complete Saviour.

To embrace Christian faith without showing Christian fruit is like the fig tree with nothing but leaves.

To preach Free Grace and to minimize or neglect good works is not to preach the full Gospel of Christ.

1. Why are good works insufficient for Justification?
2. Are good works required?
3. Name good works in which a Christian delights.
4. What does Roman Catholicism teach about good works?
5. What are works of supererogation?
6. Shall we sin, then, that grace may abound?
7. Were we created unto good works? Eph. 2:10
8. How are good works rewarded?
9. Why does this teaching prevent us from living carelessly?
10. What fruits must implantation into Christ bring forth?

# Faith and the Means of Grace

QUESTION 65 — *Since then we are made partakers of Christ and all his benefits by faith only, whence doth this faith proceed?*

ANSWER — From the Holy Ghost, who works faith in our hearts by the preaching of the Gospel, and confirms it by the use of the sacraments.

●

Faith, that all-important Christian requisite, bears a unique relation to the means of grace, which are also necessary in our religion.

Investigating this relationship we learn:

1. *What Faith Is Meant.* The very question makes that plain: "that faith which makes us partakers of Christ and all his benefits." Saving faith, therefore. Viewed in the light of the means of grace, do we see that faith in its implanation, in its unconscious state, or faith in its fruition, when we consciously embrace the promises of God contained in the Gospel? Selecting faith in its implantation, you become confused with the purpose of the Lord's Supper. Should you insist on faith in its fruition, you get in difficulty with Holy Baptism. Surely both are meant.

2. *Whence That Faith Proceeds.* From the Holy Spirit. How wonderful is God's way for sinners! Not only that Christ is God's unspeakable gift, but the very apprehension of that gift, faith, is also his gift (Eph. 2:8). By the preaching of the Gospel the Holy Spirit sowed the seed of faith in Lydia's opened heart; inclined Paul's will; enlightened Thomas' mind. So be it unto us!

3. *How That Faith Is Confirmed.* By use of the sacraments (B. Conf. 33, Canons of Dort 5:14). A correction by way of addition is in order: the Word is also used for our confirmation. Inasmuch as the sacraments are here emphasized, meager space is given to the Word, so that only two questions are devoted to the Word and fifteen to the sacraments. Were we to rewrite the Catechism today that proportion would be different. We need both Word and sacraments as means of grace for the confirmation of our faith.

4. *Who Confirms That Faith.* The Holy Spirit gives and also confirms that faith through the means of grace. This is the very heart of the matter. Here we are disturbed by the roar of lions on both sides of the way, like Christian encountered on his journey to the Heavenly City. On the one hand you hear the roar of Rome, when this church so insistently asserts that the means of

grace are the means of the Church: the Church gives or with-holds the means of grace and its benefits. Then the Church gives or withholds salvation! What a devouring and devastating claim! On the other side is the noise of those who belittle the means of grace and do without them. Do we dare go forward? Which side will devour us? The Lord has delivered us from these lions, when we believe that the means of grace are the means of the Holy Spirit. The Church administers the sacraments, but the Holy Spirit confirms our faith. The Church preaches the Gospel, but the Holy Spirit converts the soul. We cannot bind God's mercy and grace by human institutions, not even the Church! Our God is not bound by means, not even by the means of grace! But by his sovereign will he willed the means of grace, both Word and sacraments, which we may and must use. But he kept the power of confirmation in his own hand!

We march forward unafraid; we still hear the roar of the lions, but the lions are chained!

1. What kind of faith makes us partakers of Christ?
2. Who instills that faith into the believer?
3. Does the Holy Spirit confirm that faith?
4. By what means does the Holy Spirit confirm this faith?
5. Is the Word a means of grace?
6. How are sacraments means of grace?
7. Who maintain that the means of grace are confirmed by the Church?
8. Who minimize the means of grace of the sacraments?
9. Is the use of the means of grace optional?

## Sacraments: Signs and Seals

QUESTION 66 — *What are the sacraments?*

ANSWER — The sacraments are holy, visible signs and seals appointed of God for this end, that by the use thereof, he may the more fully declare and seal unto us the promise of the Gospel, viz: that he grants us freely the remission of sin and life eternal, for the sake of that one sacrifice of Christ accomplished on the cross.

●

Sacrament, a word of universal coinage in every language of Christendom, is not a Biblical word, but comes to us from Bible times and customs. In its original use it referred to the soldier's solemn oath of allegiance, and the token which was received in return. As such it was sacred, holy, as the word *sacrament* implies. In our Christian religion sacraments are tokens, signs, of allegiance also. Sacraments are:

1. *Holy Signs.* Holy, in the real meaning of that word, for they are instituted by Christ and "appointed of God." It is in that special sense, then, that we appropriately speak of and earnestly plead for the appellation "holy" when we are referring to the sacraments as *Holy* Baptism and *Holy* Supper.

2. *Visible Signs.* Signs are symbols of ready interpretation of direction and values. Road-signs, trademarks, uniforms, cattle brands, our flag and the wedding ring are valued secular illustrations. Our Christian religion has an untold number of signs. Our children see them etched on our Church windows: the cross and the crown and the cup; the shepherd's staff and the star; the lamb and the loaf, to which we would like to add the towel and yoke. Christianity was introduced by the sign of the manger. The Bible speaks of the rainbow and the stars in the sky and the sand on the seashore, sacrifices, the Sabbath, circumcision, as signs. This by no means exhausted list is mentioned to show that God uses them, and in order to counteract somewhat the efforts of those who spiritualize the sacraments and have no visible signs in their church worship.

But no matter how valuable signs may be in secular life; no matter how informative they may be in religious life, none can even faintly compare with the sacraments, for they are signs that speak to us of God's grace in Christ; the broken body and poured out blood of our Saviour; the remission of sin and eternal life. Do we hold them in such high esteem?

3. *Seals.* Now seals are different. Seals are signs too, insofar as they can be readily interpreted. They differ insofar as they are exclusive property, used for a specific purpose; only the King can attach the royal seal. Neither our county nor our federal government permits others to use its seal. The tomb was sealed. The believers are sealed unto the day of redemption. The 144 thousand were sealed. The seal first, gives assurance of authenticity; second, lends authority; third, and therefore confirms its claims and contents. Belgic Conf. 37.

But no matter how important seals may be in documents; no matter what peace treaties may be sealed by the Great Seal of the government; no matter what royal seal was ever attached to a criminal's pardon, none is greater than the sacrament by which the King of Kings seals unto us the promises of the Gospel.

How we should appreciate and long for the sacraments as signs and seals! Some believers consider Holy Baptism as "customary" and Holy Supper as "obligatory." By comparison with other tokens, may the sacraments again occupy that high place in our spiritual evaluation as divinely instituted, holy, visible signs and seals.

1. Define sacraments.
2. Whence is the word sacrament derived?
3. Of what are sacraments tokens in our Christian religion?
4. Why are sacraments holy signs?
5. Why are they visible signs?
6. Why are sacraments seals?
7. Why are they superior to all other signs and seals?
8. Is it sufficient to consider the sacraments customary or obligatory?

## Word and Sacraments

QUESTION 67 — *Are both Word and sacraments then ordained and appointed for this end, that they may direct our faith to the sacrifice of Jesus Christ on the cross, as the only ground of our salvation?*

ANSWER — Yes, indeed; for the Holy Ghost teaches us in the Gospel, and assures us by the sacraments, that the whole of our salvation depends upon that one sacrifice of Christ, which he offered for us on the cross.

If objection is made that this question is similar to the answer of the 65th question then it may be pointed out, that in the 65th answer the Holy Spirit is using both Word and sacraments "to work a faith in our hearts"; and that here the Holy Spirit uses both Word and sacraments to point that faith to "the sacrifice of Christ on the cross."

Since both Word and sacraments are "ordained and appointed" to that end, the importance of both is implied, and the continuance of both is assured. Hence they have much in common: their divine origin; their use by the Holy Spirit; their central teaching of the cross.

And they are both continuous. Some signs were temporary like the dove in the Ark and like the tongues at Pentecost. Some signs were changed, like circumcision. That can never happen to the Word and the sacraments. True, in some instances minor details of the sacraments were altered: fish was used instead of bread, for fish was the people's only food, but the true meaning was not changed.

Having all this in common, Word and sacraments differ first in their approach. The Word comes to us through the gate of our *ear*: "Hear and your soul shall live." The sacraments come largely through the gate of our *eye*. Second, in their effect: the Word is for the implantation and confirmation of our faith: the sacraments are for the confirmation only. Third, in their necessity: the way of salvation is impossible without the Word; the sacraments are not essential to salvation.

If this is so, then two questions demand our attention:

1. *Why, then does the Catechism emphasize the sacraments, instead of the Word?*

Omitting reasons of historical origin, we note that the aim of the Catechism is not to prove the Bible to be the Word of God. The Confession does that. The Catechism is a jeweler's display, attractive to the eye, so that we may "covet earnestly the best gifts." You do not have to dig the ore. The Catechism is a baker's window filled with wholesome bread. It is not a flour mill, it is not a laboratory, nor a scientist's test-tube; hence it does not concern itself about the authenticity, authority, inspiration, higher criticism, etc., of the Bible. As the hand of the Teacher guides the child's finger down the sacred page, showing its truth and beauty, its love and grace, its righteousness and holiness, and takes them all as genuine gifts of our heavenly Father without doubt or hesitation, so the Catechism proceeds from the standpoint that you believe the Bible to be the Word of God. No further defense or emphasis is needed.

2. *But why use sacraments, then, if the Word is sufficient?*

Our Confession in Art. 33 states that it is because God deemed them necessary for us on account of our weakness and waywardness. That answer suffices us, for we know that we are weak and wayward.

Hence to minimize the use of the sacraments is to question God's wisdom; to use them sincerely, faithfully and thankfully is to seek God's favor.

1. To what is our faith directed in both Word and sacrament?
2. What do Word and sacrament have in common?
3. How do they differ in approach, effect and necessity?
4. Why are the sacraments here emphasized?
5. Should we read and search the Scriptures?
6. Of what value is the ministration of the Word for the believer?
7. Of what value is the ministration of the Word for the unconverted?
8. Is the Word sufficient for our salvation, without the sacraments?
9. Why, then, use the sacraments?

# Two Sacraments

QUESTION 68 — *How many sacraments has Christ instituted in the new covenant, or testament?*

ANSWER — Two, namely, Holy Baptism, and the Holy Supper.

●

Remembering the definition of the sacraments, as holy, visible signs and seals instituted of God to more fully declare and seal unto us the promise of the Gospel, we can readily see that no Church, Synod, Pope, nor any Ecclesiastical body can add to or detract from their number.

In the Old Testament two sacraments are commanded by God. Circumcision was a sign of the Covenant that God established between himself and Abraham and his seed. According to Romans 4:11 that was a "seal of the righteousness of the faith, which he had being yet uncircumcised." The Passover was a memory of past redemption from Egypt and future salvation through the Messiah. I Cor. 5:7 teaches us: "For even Christ our passover is sacrificed for us."

These two sacraments are closely connected with the two our Lord Jesus Christ instituted, namely Holy Baptism and Holy Communion. Inasmuch as Christ is our perfect sacrifice, the sacraments are no longer bloody performances nor legal administrations, but signs and seals to teach and assure us that our salvation depends on him, who (Hebrews 10:9) "taketh away the first, that he may establish the second." Some Protestants and all Roman Catholics differ from this interpretation.

Not considering those Protestants who hold the spiritual interpretation, and as such have no visible sacraments, some mention footwashing as another sacrament. Footwashing may be literally or figuratively interpreted, but in neither case does footwashing declare and seal unto us salvation through Christ's sacrifice, and thus it is no sacrament. If we have such vague ideas that all sacred acts are sacraments, then *prayer* could qualify, and *giving* as an act of worship might be included, and many others besides.

The Bible gives us two sacraments and two are sufficient. When sacraments pertain to strengthening of saving faith, then our spiritual life, like our physical existence, needs maintenance and growth, which is the aim of Holy Baptism and the Holy Supper, and no more are needed.

But the Roman Catholic Church, which claims the power to give or withhold the sacraments and the right to deny or convey spiritual grace (which the Holy Spirit does, and no one else), adds five sacraments more. It is quite interesting that no Roman Catholic receives all seven, for *marriage* is not for the clergy and *ordination* is not for the laity. *Confirmation* is the conscious acceptance of baptismal promises but no special grace is given by the Bishop, and hence is no sacrament. *Penance* even lacks the sign of a sacrament, and also lacks divine commandment. *Ordination* is no sacrament since no grace is transmitted by the laying on of hands. *Marriage,* even though it is divinely instituted, is limited to this world, and hence is no sacrament. *Extreme unction,* based on James 5:14, was meant as oil for healing and not to sanctify the dying.

Rejecting these Roman Catholic errors, may we more faithfully adhere to and more profitably use the two sacraments which Jesus instituted (Matthew 28:19 and 26:26), namely Holy Baptism and Holy Supper.

1. What two sacraments did Jesus institute?
2. To what Old Testament sacraments do they compare?
3. How did the O.T. sacraments differ as to subjects? Form?
4. Is a spiritual interpretation of the sacraments sufficient?
5. Why is not every sacred act a sacrament?
6. How many sacraments are there in the Roman Catholic Church?
7. Why do we reject them?
8. What are the benefits for our faith in the use of the sacraments?

## Holy Baptism and Sacramental Truths

QUESTION 69 — *How art thou admonished and assured by holy baptism, that the one sacrifice of Christ upon the cross is of real advantage to thee?*

ANSWER — Thus, that Christ appointed this external washing with water, adding thereto this promise, that I am as certainly washed by his blood and Spirit from all the pollution of my soul, that is, from all my sins, as I am washed externally with water, by which the filthiness of the body is commonly washed away.

●

Clear cut, and brilliant like a summer sun, is this simple admonition and glorious assurance pertaining to holy baptism. In spite of endless equivocations and fruitless disputations, these truths stand like stone :—

1. *That Christ appointed this external washing with water.* Matt. 28:19 and Mark 16:16 are the special passages in Holy Writ referred to. The Office for Baptism, our Confession in Article 34 and the Administration itself — all are based on this fact. Since Jesus did not give us the precise form of procedure we must depend on the historical meaning of the word *baptize* as well as on the customary practice of the day. Without controversy, the Greek word means "deep" so that immersionists may have a point. Our Liturgy admits as much by speaking of "dipping in or sprinkling," and consequently holds immersion as well as sprinkling as acceptable. However the customary practice of the Old Testament was by sprinkling. Moses sprinkled the book and the people. The High Priest sprinkled the Mercy Seat. John the Baptist, trained in Old Testament custom and ceremony, baptized, and no innovation of method is mentioned.

2. *That Christ's blood and spirit washes me from the pollution of my soul.* The traveler's feet were washed as an act of hospitality. Aaron was ordered to wash his flesh with water before putting on his holy garments (Lev. 16:4). The Laver expressed a similar spiritual necessity. All this and more taught the much-needed lesson that like filthiness of the body is washed away by water, so our souls need cleansing too, for there are natural laws in the spiritual world. Dirt is our enemy. We have, we are dust, and unto dust we shall return. But meanwhile we aim to put up a good fight now that an age of hygiene and microscopic revelation verifies the ancient wisdom. The dust and germ laden atmosphere will be our undoing; civilizations have been buried under the dust of the ages. To fight this dirt which defiles and ultimately means death and despair, is the exact picture of the soul which lives in the atmosphere of evil ideas and ideals, and inhales the thoughts and suggestions, the schemes and devices of the world and the devil. We cannot keep clean in such evil surroundings. We need cleansing. "The blood of Jesus Christ, his Son, cleanseth us from all sin." "Wash me, and I shall be whiter than snow." That is God's promise and that is our prayer.

3. *That Christ assures us of this cleansing in Holy Baptism.* Now Baptism does not merely picture or represent the need for our soul's cleansing, but through the Holy Spirit we are assured of the fact that we are washed by Christ's blood and Spirit from the pollution of our soul. When baptized in the name of the blessed Trinity, we have that three-fold assurance from God the

Father as the Covenant God, from God the Son as the Mediator, and from God the Spirit who enables us to appropriate it.

1. Where did Jesus institute the sacrament of Baptism?
2. Was sprinkling practiced in the Old Testament?
3. Did Jesus give us the precise form of procedure?
4. Do we recognize immersion, if the Baptism is in the name of the Trinity?
5. What does Baptism signify for my soul?
6. Are we in need of cleansing?
7. How does Christ's blood and Spirit cleanse our soul?
8. Is this merely signified or assured?
9. If Christ cleanses us, why are we baptized in the name of God the Father, the Son and the Holy Spirit?

## Holy Baptism and Sacramental Grace (A)

QUESTION 70 — *What is it to be washed with the blood and Spirit of Christ?*

ANSWER — It is to receive of God the remission of sins freely, for the sake of Christ's blood, which he shed for us by his sacrifice upon the cross: and also to be renewed by the Holy Ghost, and sanctified to be members of Christ, that so we may more and more die unto sin, and lead holy and unblamable lives.

●

Here we are not left in the darkness concerning the significance of human ceremony or divine grace in Holy Baptism. "Sanctified to be members of Christ" leaves no room for disputes about ceremonial superficialities but places us in the light of the grace of the Triune God as it comes to us from the cross.

"What is it to be washed with the blood and Spirit of Christ?" In other words: What happens at Baptism? What grace is received? God's promise is that in connection with the appropriate use of Holy Baptism the Holy Spirit works grace in the heart of the recipient. However, the probe goes deeper when we observe that Baptism is not repeated, and so the inference must be that this sacramental grace needs no repetition. More complicated becomes this baptismal grace when grace with the Word comes again and again: "line upon line, precept upon precept." The Holy Supper is celebrated repeatedly and the accompanying grace is sought and received whenever it is observed. What is this baptismal grace?

It is almost impossible to extricate oneself from the entanglement of popular misconceptions concerning this grace of Baptism. Some advocate "baptismal regeneration," while others go to the other extreme and speak of Baptism as a mere reminder of God's promise; incorporated into the Church; an act of obedience on the part of the adult; confirmation of the covenant for the infant; even the giving of a name; the duty of instruction on the part of the Church; encouragement for the child to confess the name of the Saviour — and many more. Some of these may be interesting "by-products," but do not express sacramental grace that makes Baptism a sacrament.

What sacramental grace is received and if the Holy Spirit works that grace, why is that grace not repeated? Eph. 4:5, "One Lord, one faith, one baptism," states the fact and I Cor. 12:13 gives the explanation: "For by one spirit are we all baptized into one body." In the Catechism it is summed up in the expression "sanctified to be members of Christ." That means: Our discontinuance under the headship of Adam through our original sin. Our Liturgy expresses this in the phrase "guilty before God," which statement caused considerable discussion in our Reformed Church a few years ago. But it still remains there, and rightly so. Our Confession Art. 15 states that in Holy Baptism not all our original sin is wiped out, but that in Baptism we are freed from its condemnation. The connection with Adam is severed, once and forever through God's grace. Former Liturgies of our Church contained reference to Noah's flood in the prayer, and our Confession still retains the reference to Pharaoh's death in the Red Sea, symbolizing our escape from sin and the devil (I Peter 3:20). The deliverance from the headship of Adam is the first part of sacramental grace in Holy Baptism.

1. What happens at Baptism?
2. What does it mean to be washed with the blood and Spirit of Christ?
3. Why is Baptism not repeated like the Holy Supper?
4. Why do we reject baptismal regeneration?
5. What "by-products" of Baptism are often emphasized?
6. What sacramental grace is received?
7. Who is now our Head?

# Holy Baptism and Sacramental Grace (B)

QUESTION 70 — *What is it to be washed with the blood and Spirit of Christ?*

ANSWER — It is to receive of God the remission of sins freely, for the sake of Christ's blood, which he shed for us in his sacrifice upon the cross; and also to be renewed by the Holy Ghost, and sanctified to be members of Christ, that so we may more and more die unto sin and lead holy and unblamable lives.

●

To be delivered from the Headship of Adam, that is one grace at Baptism which needs no repetition. But the second part, or rather the counterpart, of that same grace is that we are "sanctified to be members of Christ"; in other words, that Baptism sets aside, sets apart, and includes the baptized under the Headship of Christ. So our Liturgy asks in the first question, "Do you acknowledge . . . that they are sanctified in Christ?" And our Belgic Confession 34 quotes Col. 2:11: "by the circumcision of Christ." Now our allegiance is openly shown to be to Christ, the Captain of our Salvation. That grace needs no repetition, as we are warned in our Belgic Confession 34: "that when we are baptized, we need not be baptized again as the heresy of some is." That same article teaches us that this grace is beneficial not only as long as the water of Baptism is upon us, but all the rest of our lives. In that new relationship there is remission of sin for the sake of Christ's blood, of which Baptism is the sign and seal.

Hence our Liturgy speaks as plain as day, that "as members of the Church they ought to be baptized," so that we are not baptized to become members of the Church. The adult convert is that because of his faith, and the infant of the believer on the basis of the Covenant.

Nor are we caught in the heretical quicksands of creating new spiritual life at Baptism. Roman Catholics and Lutherans have that conception but the Reformed Faith holds that Baptism is not the birth of faith and that baptismal grace did not cause the "regeneration and renewal of the Holy Spirit" but reveals, seals and enriches it.

At times it would seem that converted heathen people grasp the implication of this sacramental grace more readily, when they receive training, medical aid, benevolences that the missionaries may bring, but to the very end object to Baptism, which for them has the clear meaning of breaking with the past, and the acceptance of new leadership under Christ. Still for us, trained in the Christian religion, two questions are important:

1. *Can we be saved without baptismal grace?* Many Christians are disturbed by this and have their children baptized immediately, even by the laity in case of necessity. We believe that we can be saved without Baptism, for sacraments are not essential to salvation.

2. *Can we receive that grace without Baptism?* Yes, even if the child dies in infancy or an adult before Baptism is possible, they can receive that grace, for sacraments are for this world, and a person translated to heavenly glory receives heavenly grace where faith will be sight.

See the bride and the groom. Before the marriage vows made them one, there was the relationship of love. The wedding did not originate that love, but that ceremony revealed it and confirmed it in all its riches and fullness. Such a marriage need not be repeated and lasts for life. So in Baptism there is a relationship of faith. In Baptism that relationship of Christ and the soul is signified and sealed. That baptismal grace need not be repeated and remains with us throughout our life.

1. What does it mean to be "sanctified to be members of Christ"?
2. How does our Liturgy connect this with Baptism?
3. Are we baptized to become members of the Church?
4. On what basis is the adult baptized?
5. On what basis is the infant baptized?
6. Who teach that spiritual life is created at Baptism?
7. Can we be saved without baptismal grace?
8. Can we receive that grace without Baptism?

## Holy Baptism and Sacramental Authority

QUESTION 71 — *Where has Christ promised us, that he will as certainly wash us by his blood and Spirit, as we are washed with the water of Baptism?*

ANSWER — In the institution of Baptism, which is thus expressed: "Go ye therefore, and teach all nations, baptizing them in the name of the Father, and of the Son, and of the Holy Ghost." "He that believeth, and is baptized, shall be saved, but he that believeth not shall be damned." This promise is also repeated, where the Scripture calls Baptism "the washing of regeneration, and the washing away of sins."

Reading these words of Jesus, we are at once reminded that they form part of the Great Commission to make disciples of all nations, and to baptize those that believe. Bearing this in mind, we will see in these authoritative words of Jesus no argument against infant Baptism, since they are meant for people of "all nations" who under the Dispensation of the Gospel have come to a conscious faith in our Saviour.

Quoting the second part: "he that believeth and is baptized shall be saved," many maintain that all must believe first before they can be baptized, which they argue children cannot do. But no chronological order of believing and Baptism is intended, for then it should read "shall be baptized." To remain literal one may interpret "is baptized" as referring to the past: "has been baptized."

Also the reference to Titus 3:5, "by the washing of regeneration," is not meant to emphasize the method but the meaning of Baptism, witness verse 7: "that being justified by his grace," not by a certain preferred method of Baptism.

Aside from these and other little foxes that destroy the vineyard of Christian harmony, the sacraments must again be upheld in the light of sacramental authority. We are in danger of humanizing divine institutions, and Holy Baptism commonly suffers from those of its own household.

There is reason for that danger. This authoritative command of Jesus is preceded by his words: "All power is given to me in heaven and earth." Now this glorious, exalted Christ commands a most ordinary element as a sign and a seal of his grace! Little wonder that many Christians ask: Is not faith in that wonderful Saviour sufficient? Why must I submit to such an elementary ceremony? Maybe it is necessary for ignorant believers, or for those whose superstition attributes hidden powers to mysterious performances, but we worship God in spirit and in truth: these church ceremonies do not save us, and our faith in the crucified Saviour is sufficient for us. So they say.

These are days when we need a renewed emphasis on sacramental authority. Shall the creature say to its Maker: Why hast thou made me so? Why did God give you a body, when the soul is of supreme importance? Why were you created needing food, clothing, medicine, while angels were created spirits?

The fact remains that we need means for physical sustenance, health and growth, and in God's wisdom certain blessings of spiritual grace accompany definite obedience to the divine authority for the means of grace.

No cynical attitude, no hesitating obedience, but a humble and a wholehearted acceptance of the sacramental authority of Jesus brings honor to the Trinity and spiritual health and growth to the believer. I Peter 3:21, 22.

1. What does the Great Commission say about Baptism?
2. Does that exclude infants?
3. Does "he that believeth and is baptized" plead for adult Baptism?
4. What is the teaching of Titus 3:5?
5. Is there need today to emphasize the divine authority for Baptism?
6. What attitude minimizes the importance of Baptism?
7. Is private Baptism a good practice?
8. Is Baptism for God's glory as well as for the believer's health and grace?

## Holy Baptism and Sacramental Cleansing

QUESTION 72 — *Is then the external Baptism with water the washing away of sin itself?*

ANSWER — Not at all; for the blood of Jesus Christ only, and the Holy Ghost, cleanse us from all sin.

QUESTION 73 — *Why then doth the Holy Ghost call Baptism "the washing of regeneration" and "the washing away of sins"?*

ANSWER — God speaks thus not without great cause, to wit, not only thereby to teach us, that as the filth of the body is purged away by water, so our sins are removed by the blood and Spirit of Jesus Christ; but especially, that by this divine pledge and sign, he may assure us that we are spiritually cleansed from our sins, as really as we are externally washed with water.

❋

"What can wash away my sin? Nothing but the blood of Jesus!" That truth so precious is plainly set forth in Question 69 and at the risk of duplication but to remove the final vestige of hesitation concerning the basic cause of sacramental cleansing in Holy Baptsm, we are in a final statement faced with:

1. *A Biblical Symbol.* The Holy Spirit calls Baptism "the washing of regeneration" and "the washing away of sins." Yes, the Bible frequently uses this expression in connection with Baptism: I Cor. 6:11: "Ye are washed"; Titus 3:5: "By the wash-

ing of regeneration"; Rev. 1:5: "And washed us from our sins in his blood." There is no doubt about it: Baptism and the washing away of sins are mentioned in one breath, and so our Liturgy: "When we are baptized into the name of the Son, God assures us of our cleansing through the blood of Christ."

2. *An Honest Question.* Is then the external Baptism with water the washing away of sin itself? From these Biblical quotations it would seem that all depended on the outward ceremony. Many still believe that. If we believe that the Church administers the sacraments and gives grace with the sacraments, then the answer is in the affirmative. But when we know that the Church administers the sacraments but that the Holy Spirit gives sacramental grace, the last trace of hesitation is removed even from our thoughts, that the water in Baptism is the washing away of sin itself.

3. *A Trustworthy Answer*: "God speaks thus not without great cause." The answer is, No, but it is not a categorical negative. We may not confuse the similarity of the symbol with the water of Baptism and the blood of Christ, but God uses that similarity to teach us certain fundamental truths. In these Bible passages God speaks to us:

A. To point out our need of spiritual cleansing.
B. To direct us to the blood and Spirit of Christ.
C. To assure us of the reality of our spiritual cleansing.

So I Peter 3:21 reminds us of the story of Noah who was not saved because of the water, but from the water and in the ark. And the Israelites passing through the Red Sea had a consciousness of safety not while passing through the water but when they were saved from the water. So it is not the water of Baptism that saves, but when we are baptized the Holy Spirit applying Jesus' blood for our salvation gives us the assurance that he to whom we now belong was able to save and is able to keep.

1. Does Baptism wash way sin?
2. Are there Biblical expressions symbolizing washing away of sin?
3. Does cleansing come through Baptism or the Holy Spirit?
4. Do we need spiritual cleansing?
5. What do you mean by the "washing of regeneration"?
6. What only can wash away our sin?
7. How are we assured of spiritual cleansing?
8. Do we advocate baptizing by any one in extremities?

# Holy Baptism and Sacramental Subjects

QUESTION 74 — *Are infants also to be baptized?*

ANSWER — Yes, for since they, as well as the adult, are included in the covenant and Church of God; and since redemption from sin by the blood of Christ, and the Holy Ghost, the author of faith, is promised to them no less than to the adult: they must, therefore, by Baptism, as a sign of the covenant, be also admitted into the Christian Church, and be distinguished from the children of infidels, as was done in the old covenant, or testament, by circumcision, instead of which Baptism is instituted in the new covenant.

●

Infants of believing parents are proper subjects for Holy Baptism, since they are included in the covenant of God. Belgic Confession 35. Canon 1:17. Infant Baptism stands or falls with our faith in or rejection of the covenant of grace. These covenantal truths we hold to be Biblical and essential and final reasons for infant Baptism:

1. *There is a covenant of God in our Christian Dispensation.* There was an old covenant made with Abraham. A new covenant was promised, Ez. 31:31. Jesus assures us of the fulfillment of that promise: Matt. 26:28. "This is my blood of the new testament," or covenant.

2. *Children were included in the old and are included in the new covenant.* I Cor. 7:14: "Else were your children unclean, but now they are holy." Our Liturgy quotes Peter's statement: "The promise is unto you and your children" and Jesus' example: "He laid his hands on them and blessed them." Canon 1:17 emphasizes this in connection with the Doctrine of Election.

3. *There was a sign of the covenant in the old and there is a sign of the covenant in the new.* Col. 2:11 speaks of the "circumcision of Christ and buried with him in baptism." Belgic Confession 34. Infant Baptism is not merely a dedication ceremony on the part of the parents: it is an acceptation and confirmation of the promise of God — the divine side of the covenant — for the coming generation, and Baptism of the child is of that the sign and the seal.

The baptismal font should occupy a prominent and permanent place. Infant Baptism should never be looked upon as something not quite so "impressive" or "wonderful" as adult Baptism, when the church rejoices in the Baptism of the adult who has confessed his faith in our Saviour. Infant Baptism should not suffer by way of diminished interest or joy. The reason is plain. In adult baptism the one who is baptized or the Church might think of the person first. Not so in infant Baptism. Here God's grace stands first and foremost. Here the infant is unaware of its need and unable to supply. Here its very helplessness points to the grace of God first of all. And that is where our minds and hearts belong. In the Holy Supper we are to "believe," to "take," to "remember" to "examine"; all expressing personal activity calling attention to self. Holy Baptism of the infant has none of these; it rests in God's promise and that is its glory.

In infant Baptism the child receives the sign and the seal of the covenant of grace; the parents accept the promise of God, and the church witnesses confirmation of the covenant. And the angels? Would they be interested in the child at Baptism? When Jesus said that their angels always behold the face of his Father, they welcome their new charge, but marvel most of all at the comprehensive, condescending grace of the covenant God.

1. Who are subjects of Baptism?
2. Are adults baptized without confession of faith?
3. Why are infants baptized?
4. What is the relation between the Covenant of grace and our children?
5. Was there an old covenant and a new covenant?
6. Were children included in both covenants?
7. What was the sign of the covenant in the O. T. and in the N. T.?
8. Is adult Baptism more impressive?
9. What is the part of the believing parents?

# The Lord's Supper and Sacramental Symbolism

QUESTION 75 — *How art thou admonished and assured in the Lord's Supper, that thou art a partaker of that one sacrifice of Christ, accomplished on the cross, and of all his benefits?*

ANSWER — Thus, that Christ has commanded me, and all believers, to eat of this broken bread, and to drink of this cup in remembrance of him; adding these promises, first, that his body was offered and broken on the cross for me, and his blood shed for me, as certainly as I see with my eyes, the bread of the Lord broken for me, and the cup communicated to me; And further, that he feeds and nourishes my soul to everlasting life, with his crucified body and shed blood, as assuredly as I receive from the hands of the minister, and taste with my mouth, the bread and cup of the Lord, as certain signs of the body and blood of Christ.

●

Christ, in his sacrificial death, left no mighty monument to perpetuate, no marble mausoleum to adorn, no beautiful temple to contemplate his undying love. Yet he gave us a simple memorial in the Lord's Supper, like a friend we love gives a ring, that looking at it we may be reminded of our mutual vows. Considering this institution of the Lord's Supper, let us here study its symbolism, in: —

A. *Its Name*. Would that we had one definite name for this sacrament! In Question 68: "Holy Supper" is used and here we are asked concerning the "Lord's Supper." Jesus designated this institution by the expression: "Blood of the New Testament." Turning to Acts 2:45 and Acts 20:7 we find "the breaking of bread." I Cor. 10:21 deals with the distinction between the "cup of the Lord" and the cup of devils: and also mentions "the Lord's table." I Cor. 11:20 speaks of the "Lord's Supper," and in verse 26: "this bread," and "this cup." I Cor. 10:16 has the name "Communion." For the disciples it was at the time of the Passover, and Paul writes, I Cor. 5:17, "Even Christ our passover is sacrificed for us." Now when the Passover has transcended national significance and boundaries, every name recorded is still symbolical of the Paschal lamb and the Paschal meal recording the freedom from Egypt, the freedom from sin.

B. *Its Action*. We are to eat of this broken bread and to drink of this cup. Surely, it is in remembrance of him. But it is not left to our choice *how* we are to remember him. Not primarily his wonderful life and teaching; his forgiving spirit and power to heal, but his broken body and shed blood. We are to eat, "and the cup is communicated to me," symbolical of how he feeds and nourishes our souls to everlasting life with His crucified body and shed blood.

C. *Its Elements*. This answer states "certain signs": two signs, the bread and the cup, even though the contents of the cup are not directly stated but implied. Elements as simple and essential as life itself; elements symbolizing our need of spiritual life; elements which can sustain life, but cannot create life; so our spiritual life is to be nourished, but it is not created, pardoned, or regenerated in this sacrament. Among all the means of grace none so visibly and so forcibly expresses our need of the feeding of our spiritual life as this Holy Supper of the Lord.

1. How does the Lord's Supper assure us that we are partakers of Christ's sacrifice?
2. As we eat the bread, what promise does Christ give us?
3. As we taste with our mouth, how is our soul nourished?
4. Mention other names for the Lord's Supper.
5. What is their significance?
6. What action is symbolized?
7. What do the elements symbolize?
8. What is "close communion"?
9. What are "preparatory" services?

## The Lord's Supper and Sacramental Significance

QUESTION 76 — *What is it then to eat the crucified body and drink the shed blood of Christ?*

ANSWER — It is not only to embrace with a believing heart all the sufferings and death of Christ, and thereby to obtain the pardon of sin and life eternal; but also, besides that, to become more and more united to his sacred body by the Holy Ghost, who dwells both in Christ and in us; so that we, though Christ is in Heaven and we on earth, are, notwithstanding, "flesh of his flesh and bone of his bone"; and that we live and are governed forever by one spirit, as members of the same body are by one soul.

Simple yet significant are the two signs of bread and wine in the Lord's Supper. The question now becomes pertinent: What is it then to eat the crucified body and drink the shed blood of Christ? How is it possible for us to do that? Is it not sufficient just to display the elements? Some withhold the cup from the laity like Roman Catholics do. Many Protestants consider it an act of obedience and deny all mystery and expect no grace. What is it, then?

"To embrace with a believing heart" (a statement worthy of being engraved upon the tablets of our soul) all the sufferings and death of Christ. No, these signs are not to be accepted without participation, like we fly our flag, or to be displayed like a historical monument, but these signs are to be appropriated and their significance must be "embraced with a believing heart" as we eat the crucified body and drink the shed blood of Christ.

But how is this possible? The Jews objected to Jesus' teaching:

"How can this man give us his flesh to eat?" When Jesus speaks in John 6:51, "The bread that I will give is my flesh," he also explains in the same chapter: "The flesh profiteth nothing: the words that I speak unto you, they are spirit and they are life." As these elements become part of our physical body, so his words must become "flesh of our flesh and bone of our bone." Not just for historical information; not a mental consent, but a hearty conviction. Then the true communicant is fed with the body and blood of Christ, as Jesus said: "Take, eat, this is my body." And Paul in I Cor. 10:16: "The cup of blessing which we bless, is it not the communion of the blood of Christ?"

The literal and physical interpretation of these signs may furnish less difficulty once we believe like the Roman Catholics that the signs are "truly, essentially and really" changed into Christ's body and blood, but our forefathers in the days of the Reformation turned away from this physical representation in that impossible transformation. How happy we are, in spite of its far more difficult interpretation, that *it is to embrace with a believing heart* all the sufferings and death of Christ. To trust in the redeeming work of our Saviour: to be united to his sacred body by the Holy Spirit; and to live and be governed forever by one spirit of the Living Lord, that is "to embrace him with a believing heart" which constitutes the significance in the Lord's Supper of the sacramental signs.

1. What is the true significance of the Lord's Supper?
2. Discuss the Lord's Supper as an act of obedience, a memorial, a display.
3. Is the Lord's Supper for our conversion?
4. How and when are these signs of the Lord's Supper appropriated?
5. How do we embrace the suffering of Christ?
6. How does the Holy Spirit increase our union with Christ?
7. If a physical interpretation is easier, is it Biblical?
8. What is Jesus own interpretation of his flesh? (John 6)

## The Lord's Supper and Sacramental Sources

QUESTION 77 — *Where has Christ promised that he will as certainly feed and nourish believers with his body and blood, as they eat of this broken bread, and drink of this cup?*

ANSWER — In the institution of the Supper, which is thus expressed: "The Lord Jesus, the same night in which he was betrayed, took bread, and when he had given thanks, he brake it, and said, Take, eat; this is my body which is broken for you; this do in remembrance of me: after the same manner also he took the cup, when he had supped, saying, This cup is the new testament in my blood; this do ye, as oft as ye drink it, in remembrance of me. For, as often as ye eat this bread, and drink this cup, ye do show the Lord's death till he come." This promise is repeated by the holy apostle Paul, where he says: "The cup of blessing which we bless, is it not the communion of the blood of Christ? The bread which we break, is it not the communion of the body of Christ? for we, being many, are one bread and one body, because we are all partakers of that one bread."

●

One of the requisites of a sacrament is its divine institution. No fleeting dream nor passing fancy furnish the basis of the institution of the Lord's Supper. Its solid foundation is found in the words of our Lord in the three Gospels, and its blessed promises are repeated by the holy apostle Paul, indicated above.

The Lord's Supper is *Divinely Instituted*. In addition to these Bible references, this is evident from the name: the Lord's Supper, when we emphasize "the Lord's." It is not the Church, nor the minister, nor the congregation who invite us: it is the Lord's Supper at the Lord's table. Likewise when we say: Holy Supper, it is not so named because it arouses holy emotions, not because the elements are holy, but because it comes to us from a holy God.

The Lord's Supper is *Divinely Provided*. Come, for all things are ready. All we are asked is to come by faith, for like in Abraham's sacrifice, our perfect Lamb of God is freely given. One thing always to hold in view in a sacrament is not what we do for God, but what God does for us. It is not first of all what the Church does; nor what the minister says, nor what the participant expects; it is what God did for us and does for us and does in us. Now in contrast with all other means of grace, none so vividly and forcibly expresses the feeding of our soul upon the broken body and shed blood of Christ, as these elements in the Lord's Supper.

The Lord's Supper is *Divinely Designated*. Expressions like table, Supper, bread, cup, designate not an altar, nor sacrifice, but a table. The Holy Supper is the Lord's *Table,* not a form of an altar, nor a place of an altar, nor steps to an altar. We do not kneel at the altar rail; we sit at a table around which the minister and elders and the whole congregation gather. This divine designation of a table needs emphasis in our day, for some Churches have lost this significance. Yet the distinctive joy and precious heritage of the Reformation was the restoration of the Communion Table. It is his body and his blood at his table. The feeding and refreshing of our soul is symbolized by eating and drinking at a table.

The Lord's Supper is *Divinely Perpetuated*. "Until he come." As the Passover for the Jew was a perpetual national institution, so we are commanded as often as we eat this bread and drink this cup to show the Lord's death, until he comes. Or in Jesus' words (Matt. 26:29) : "Until that day when I drink it new with you in my Father's kingdom." Then the Lord's Supper will culminate in the Marriage Feast (Rev. 19:7) : "Let us be glad and rejoice, and give honor to him, for the marriage of the Lamb is come." Blessed communion with Christ and the believers! Praise his name, we shall see him face to face, if we are faithful "until he comes."

1. Where is the Institution of the Lord's Supper found in the Gospels and in the Epistles?
2. What is the significance of the name **Lord's** Supper, and the meaning of **Holy** in Holy Supper?
3. Is the Lord's Supper divinely provided?
4. Is the form divinely designated?
5. What alterations have some made in its form?
6. Do we have a divine rule for its perpetuation?
7. When partaking do we have Christ's return in mind?
8. What will be the culmination of the Lord's Supper?

## The Lord's Supper and Sacramental Substance

QUESTION 78 — *Do then the bread and wine become the very body and blood of Christ?*

ANSWER — Not at all, but as the water in Baptism is not changed into the blood of Christ, neither is the washing away of sin itself, being only the sign and confirmation thereof appointed of God; so the bread in the Lord's Supper is not changed into the very body of Christ, though agreeably to the nature and properties of sacraments, it is called the body of Christ Jesus.

●

Clearing up the muddy waters of misinterpretation and superstition is not a task of pure delight, but sheer necessity compels us here to consider "what this sacrament is not" and to learn in the next answer "what this sacrament is."

Negatively considered, then, we reject the Roman Catholic and Lutheran error of a change in the substance of the element in the Lord's Supper. In Baptism the water did not change into the blood of Christ and so the bread in the Lord's Supper is not changed into the very body of Christ.

Roman Catholics believe that the substance of the bread is changed at the words of the priest into the real, actual body of Christ; this is the heresy of transubstantiation. Lutherans maintain the same change "in, with and under" the participation of the believers; this is consubstantiation.

We believe in the spiritual presence of Christ and the body and blood of Christ are received by faith, "which (Conf. Art. 35) is the hand and the mouth of our soul." The error of their miraculous deception is proved by:

1. *The Physical Argument.* The substance, identity, of the bread is not changed. It still looks like and tastes like bread, for it remains bread, as our senses tell us. And poisoned bread would not turn into harmless substance.

2. *The Logical Argument.* Since the greater includes the lesser, the inability to do small miracles of healing proves the false claim of doing this tremendous miracle of changing bread into God.

3. *Biblical Theology.* Transubstantiation is overthrown by the very conception of a sacrament, which always is a sign and never a reality. When it is pronounced a reality, it is no longer a sacrament. Furthermore, theologically considered, the whole teaching of Christ's ascension and of his glorified body must be interpreted contrary to Scripture, which they do when they confess that "he ascended into heaven" and then make the impossible claim that they have re-created his physical body back here on earth.

4. *Biblical Interpretations.* When Jesus said, "I am the door," we have little difficulty in understanding that the verb used allows no literal interpretation, but means, "represent." Or Jesus' own explanation in John 6:63, and God's statement to Abraham (Gen. 17:10), "This is my covenant," referring to circumcision but meaning his promise. And in addition to all this, both in Gen. 17:10 in the Hebrew language and in Matt. 26:26 in the Greek language, the much disputed word, *is,* on which the whole argument of transubstantiation is built, does not appear.

1. Is the bread and wine changed into the very body and blood of Christ?
2. What comparison is made with the water at Baptism?
3. What do we mean by "though agreeable to the nature and properties of sacraments"?
4. What is the Lutheran interpretation; the Roman Catholic interpretation?
5. Is that change of substance evident physically?
6. Can they who claim to be able to perform this miracle, prove it by doing lesser miracles?
7. If transubstantiation were true would it still be a sacrament?
8. Name other statements of Jesus which cannot be taken literally.

## The Lord's Supper and Sacramental Grace

QUESTION 79 — *Why then does Christ call the bread his body, and the cup his blood, or the new covenant in his blood; and Paul, the "communion of the body and blood of Christ"?*

ANSWER — Christ speaks thus not without great reason, namely, not only thereby to teach us that as bread and wine support this temporal life, so his crucified body and shed blood are the true meat and drink whereby our souls are fed to eternal life; but more especially by these visible signs and pledges to assure us, that we are as really partakers of this true body and blood (by the operation of the Holy Ghost) as we receive by the mouths of our bodies these holy signs in remembrance of him; and that all his sufferings and obedience are as certainly ours, as if we had in our own persons suffered and made satisfaction for our sins to God.

●

Having considered that the substance of the elements in the Lord's Supper is not changed, we now focus our attention on the positive blessing in the Lord's Supper as a means of grace.

No more than other means of grace, like prayer, or the ministry of the Word, are acts of grace, so the Lord's Supper is not an act of grace in itself but a channel of grace. As a channel of grace then, in what respect does the grace received differ from that received in other means of grace? If we can receive the same benefits from the Word, why observe the Lord's Supper faithfully? Is it just a repetition or intensification of the other means of grace? Or is there no grace at all, no mystery at all, like Zwingli upheld, just to refresh our minds? No, this answer states plainly that Christ does more to our soul: "that our souls are fed unto eternal life."

*Ex opera operato,* the grace received from participation regardless of faith or knowledge of the participant, is unworthy of further consideration.

No mere refresher course of the mind, nor a theatrical stirring of the emotion like the Passion Play (what horrid contradiction in terminology: Passion was not and is not play!), touch the soul like the Holy Spirit does in the Lord's Supper.

What differentiates this grace, then, from other means of grace which also give us increased faith, hope and love? Is it an emphasis in sight and taste of what we believe in our hearts? Is it an act of devotion and Christian fellowship which warms our hearts? Does it create in us a renewed sense of reverence and love for our Saviour which sets our souls aglow? Is it to see God's unspeakable gift of his Son more clearly and personally, like we always see God's hand in nature, but are at times impressed by a thunderstorm or attracted by the beauty of a blossoming spring?

Yes, it is all that and even more than that. It is the Communion with Christ's body and blood. So grace in the Lord's Supper surpasses or by-passes the words and personality of the minister and draws us to Christ; it is the communion of the soul and Christ: the soul to receive and the Holy Spirit to apply the merits of Christ.

Hence, the address must be at a minimum and may be omitted, using the words of Christ. Not even the Communion of the Saints receives the emphasis, although it is an essential consequence. Here the soul rests in God and waits patiently for him. Here we are assured, as if we in our own person had suffered and made satisfaction for our sin.

That sacramental grace is still a mystery. But how blessed this mystery is for the believing soul!

1. What sacramental grace does the participant receive?
2. Is the Lord's Supper an act or a channel of grace?
3. Is grace received without faith or knowledge?
4. Who hold that no grace is received at all?
5. Is that grace different from what is received by the ministration of the Word?
6. What does the Holy Spirit do for the partaker?
7. What should be emphasized: the Communion of the Saints or the Communion with Christ?
8. After all explanations, is there still an element of mystery?

# The Lord's Supper and Sacramental Sacrilege

QUESTION 80 — *What difference is there between the Lord's Supper and the popish mass?*

ANSWER — The Lord's Supper testifies to us, that we have a full pardon of all sin by the only sacrifice of Jesus Christ, which he himself has once accomplished on the cross; and that we, by the Holy Ghost, are ingrafted into Christ, who, according to his human nature, is now not on earth but in heaven, at the right hand of God his Father, and will there be worshiped by us: but the mass teacheth, that the living and dead have not the pardon of sins through the sufferings of Christ, unless Christ is also daily offered for them by the priests; and further that Christ is bodily under the form of bread and wine, and therefore is to be worshiped in them; so that the mass at bottom is nothing else than a denial of the one sacrifice and sufferings of Jesus Christ, and an accursed idolatry.

●

Present-day commentators feel at this point that enough has been said about Roman Catholic heresy of the Lord's Supper and so conveniently omit further reference to this question. All the more so, because the expression "popish mass" is not considered worthy of a place in our ecumenical vocabulary, and "accursed idolatry" sounds like an unkind criticism.

However, when we realize that the Catechism condemns the mass as an act of sacrilege but does not curse the priest or the worshiper, heeding Jesus' warning; but that Rome hurls its anathemas ("let him be cursed") upon people who are differently minded, we need not apologize for the truth that in the mass the creature is worshiped instead of the Creator and as such is idolatry, which is cursed of God.

"Popish" mass is not exactly accurate, for many who disclaim the pope have the mass.

The mass follows Communion in the Roman Catholic Church. The three essentials of Communion are for the Roman Catholics: 1. Offering of bread and wine. 2. Transubstantiation of these elements into the real body and blood of Christ, at the word of the priest. 3. Communion: receiving the wafer (or host, which means victim).

The mass is that ceremony where the wafer is elevated and worshiped. Even though the Latin phrases are Biblical we condemn the mass as unbiblical and sacrilegious and idolatrous. The book containing the services of the mass, the Missal, is:

1. A *misconception* of sacrament and sacrifice. Rome still includes the Communion among the sacraments, but interprets it as a sacrifice. Now either of two is true: this sacrifice is not a sacrament, or the sacrament is not a sacrifice.

2. A *misrepresentation* of spiritual benefit through physical bread, which they claim is Christ's body. But Jesus said, John 6:63, "The words that I speak unto you, they are spirit, and they are life."

3. A *misleading* of the Roman clergy. To claim this miraculous change is a lie; to believe it is contrary to reality; and to worship this supposed creature is idolatry. In preaching the Second Commandment, why do we not mention the widespread transgression of the idolatry of the mass?

4. A *misinterpretation* and denial of the complete and sufficient sacrifice of Christ. As for the Old Testament saints, where did they get salvation, if all depended on the mass? And in the New Testament Jesus said: "It is finished" after his suffering. While Hebrews 10:10, "We are sanctified through the offering of the body of Jesus Christ, once for all." And for us, the Lord's Supper points again to the only sacrifice of Christ on the cross, but the priest pretends to sacrifice the body of Christ everywhere and every day, where Rome holds sway.

When so much is at stake, it is still necessary to warn against the accursed idolatry of the popish mass.

1. Why is the mass a sacrilege?
2. Was the sacrifice of Christ complete and once for all?
3. Can that sacrifice be repeated daily in the mass?
4. May the elements be worshiped as is done in the mass?
5. Why is the cup withheld from the laity in the mass?
6. Is "accursed idolatry" too strongly expressed?
7. Distinguish sacrament from sacrifice.
8. What is the application of the Second Commandment?

# The Lord's Supper and Sacramental Subjects

QUESTION 81 — *For whom is the Lord's Supper instituted?*

ANSWER — For those who are truly sorrowful for their sins, and
yet trust that these are forgiven them for the sake of Christ;
and that their remaining infirmities are covered by his passion
and death; and who also earnestly desire to have their faith
more and more strengthened, and their lives more holy. But
hypocrites, and such as turn not to God with sincere hearts,
eat and drink judgment to themselves.

●

Illuminated by the precepts of Holy Writ, we here consider
for whom the Lord's Supper is instituted.

If we do more than merely pay lip service to the teaching of
the Scriptures, we learn that this sacrament is ordained to direct
our faith to the sacrifice of Christ on the cross. This direction of
our faith implies first of all that there is saving faith, for the Holy
Supper is not a converting sacrament, nor is it meant for our
regeneration, nor to obtain pardon. And secondly, that there is a
recognition of the needs for nourishment and maintenance of that
faith.

Hence these explicit points are stated for these communicants:
that they are truly sorrowful for their sins; that they trust in
Christ for forgiveness; that their remaining infirmities are covered
by his passion; that they are desirous for stronger faith and holy
lives.

At what age can this religious consciousness be expected?
When in the old dispensation religion and patriotism were virtually
unanimous, the youth of twelve years was through the Passover
initiated into tribal maturity. Circumcision was not an act of
self-determination, but the Passover became an expression of
personal choice and coherence with the group.

Because of this Biblical background, somewhat similar ideas
maintain among us when we consider the subjects for whom the
Lord's Supper is instituted.

Some still adhere to this national conformity when now there
is only ecclesiastical connection. Roman Catholics practice Confirmation at that stage in imitation of the youth at Passover, when
our government is no longer a theocracy. So this present day

practice does not emphasize faith but an examination in the accepted customs and rules of the Church.

We must leave no stone unturned to save our churches from the mere mental assent to doctrine without personal faith in Christ and his redemption. But we must also most assiduously guard against the opposite swing of the pendulum which restricts communicants to those of older age and then automatically commits the same error for those of sixteen years and up. Children can be sincere and earnest believers too. Yes, their faith is imperfect and weak, but the Holy Supper is meant to strengthen such faith. There are many evidences of those who are still immature in years and yet have reached a stage of spiritual apprehension. Conviction of sin is not restricted by the Spirit and at times is a powerful factor in youth.

Then I Cor. 11 speaks of self-examination and our Liturgy explains in detail *how* we must proceed in that examination. Such self-examination is essential for the individual communicant, and will prove to be a blessing for the spiritual well-being of the entire body of Christ.

1. What faith is required for the participant?
2. Is weak but true faith an objection?
3. What three requirements are necessary?
4. As at the Passover does age enter in as a requirement?
5. Is Confirmation at a certain age sufficient?
6. Is a mere consent to historical truths sufficient?
7. Is conviction of sin and faith in our Saviour essential?
8. What does our Liturgy teach about self-examination?

## The Lord's Supper and Sacramental Discipline

QUESTION 82 — *Are they also to be admitted to this Supper who, by confession and life declare themselves infidels and ungodly?*

ANSWER — No; for by this the covenant of God would be profaned, and his wrath kindled against the whole congregation; therefore it is the duty of the Christian Church, according to the appointment of Christ and his apostles, to exclude such persons, by the keys of the kingdom of heaven, till they show amendment of life.

●

No elasticity of conviction befits anyone dealing with those who by confession and life declare themselves infidels and ungodly. They are to be excluded from the Lord's Table till they show amendment of life.

Unpleasant indeed, and hence oft neglected, but not unprofitable, is this most difficult task of the Church. That the Bible furnishes sound basis for this duty — "he that eateth and drinketh unworthily" — no one can deny. And the punishment for the transgressor is plainly stated: "For this cause many are sick" (I Cor. 11:30), when Church members are unconscious of their soul's welfare.

Thus the covenant of God is profaned and the wrath of God is kindled against the whole congregation. Congregations prosper and grow but many dwindle and die. Think of the warning example of the seven churches in Revelation! Many languishing churches might well find the root of bitterness in their neglect of discipline.

For many churches exercise not even a shadow of discipline and purposely let down all bars of exclusion. Is it any wonder that such churches degenerate into social groups or fall by the wayside? It may seem and sound broad-minded to exercise no discipline, but neither the church nor the erring brother is benefited thereby. If one complains that it is difficult to maintain supervision when escape into a more liberal group is so easily accomplished, be it remembered that no matter how feeble or inadequate, God honors these efforts in order that the covenant of God may not be profaned and the wayward may be warned and be led to return to the Lord.

Exclusion by the fiat of the consistory, even of visiting believers, caused participating members to consider the approval of the consistory sufficient evidence of their sacramental right, disregarding personal responsibilities.

Proper church supervision includes: (a) The discipline of the Word, as it is preached in fidelity and purity. Preparatory sermons can be heart-searching, informative and effective. (b) The reading of the Liturgy, which is more than beautiful; it is appropriate. (c) The Office of the Elders. When becoming Elders, they have promised "to prevent, as much as possible, the Sacraments from being profaned"; the Constitutional Question is asked and recorded before each celebration of the Lord's Supper; the keys of the kingdom are in their hands. (d) Mailing communion invitations with a proper follow-up system. (e) Consistorial callings at stated times like Family Visits to encourage the weak; warn the wayward; invite those who have absented themselves or have various scruples; to remember the shut-ins, the sick, the aged. (f) And much-needed unofficial care of and interest in fellow members of the same household or of the same neighborhood as fellow believers to keep the church pure and our hearts warm, by speaking a word of testimony for our Lord, and to help the church officials.

Thank God for church discipline — for those who care for our soul! Thank God for the church that displays the Banner of Mercy, which is Justice in Tears!

1. Does our faith influence our life?
2. Are those who lead ungodly lives to be admitted to the Lord's Supper?
3. What is eating and drinking unworthily?
4. Does God honor church discipline?
5. Does the whole church suffer when this is not exercised?
6. What steps are required in discipline?
7. What is the discipline of the Word?
8. Name other means of care and discipline which Christians may exercise.
9. Should we be thankful for Sacramental Discipline?

## The Keys of the Kingdom of Heaven

(A) The Preaching of the Holy Gospel

QUESTION 83 — *What are the keys of the kingdom of heaven?*

ANSWER — The preaching of the holy Gospel, and Christian discipline, or excommunication out of the Christian Church; by these two, the kingdom of heaven is opened to believers, and shut against unbelievers.

QUESTION 84 — *How is the kingdom of heaven opened and shut by the preaching of the holy Gospel?*

ANSWER — Thus: when, according to the command of Christ, it is declared and publicly testified to all and every believer, that whenever they receive the promise of the Gospel by a true faith, all their sins are really forgiven them of God, for the sake of Christ's merits; and on the contrary, when it is declared and testified to all unbelievers, and such as do not sincerely repent, that they stand exposed to the wrath of God, and eternal condemnation, so long as they are unconverted; according to which testimony of the Gospel, God will judge them, both in this and the life to come.

●

In our Protestant circles very little knowledge and appreciation is shown of the Scripture-searching efforts and soul-stirring trials, which in the days of the Reformation pointed out the Roman Catholic fallacy of the keys of the Confessional and

Papal Ban and reformed them into the Biblical interpretation of the Preaching of the Word and Christian Discipline.

The key is the symbol of authority in the Church, like the sword is the symbol of authority in the State. Jesus gave Peter the keys of the Kingdom of heaven (Matt. 16:19). Hence Peter is generally depicted with the keys, but the Bible pictures him twice with the sword: at one time he produced two swords (Luke 22:38, on which text Rome bases its claim for authority in both Church and State) and in Gethsemane he made active use of the sword.

The keys given to Peter were also given to the other apostles (John 20:23) and they proved this authority by the power to perform miracles (Acts 3). Now the Pope claims to be the successor of Peter and claims to forgive sin, but lacks the power to perform miracles to prove this authority. If he cannot heal physically, how can he heal spiritually?

The power to heal was never handed over to the successors of the Apostles, but the Apostolic command was: Preach the Word. Hence the first key is the preaching of the Gospel.

*This key opens.* The preaching of the Gospel opens the door to the Kingdom of heaven. When forgiveness is offered for the sake of Christ's merit and when the Spirit convinces of sin the spiritual miracles occur: the blind see, the deaf hear, the lame walk, the dead live. "Repent and believe": that power of the key is on authority of the King and honored in heaven as the gates swing open. No priestly confessional and absolution, but the preaching of the Gospel is the key of the Kingdom of heaven. Canons of Dort. 3:15. Belg. Conf. Art. 32.

*This key shuts.* If the preaching of the Gospel is for the admission into the Kingdom of heaven, it follows that there is danger outside. There is, for souls must be saved from the wrath and judgment of God. Unless they repent, they are left to eternal condemnation. The Gospel is no "glad tidings" of salvation, unless it tells us what we are saved from. Thus not every speech is a sermon, nor is every flight of oratory in the pulpit a proper use of the key. Even a watered-down message of love and praise and peace, without warning and admonition to repent, is not a complete Gospel testimony. "He that believeth not shall be damned." That power of the key is honored in heaven too and even though unpopular is essential to the preaching of the Gospel, the first key of the Kingdom of heaven.

1. When does Christian discipline become personal and specific?
2. What are the keys of the kingdom of heaven?
3. What was their form before the Reformation?
4. What is their form since the Reformation?
5. Of what is the key the symbol?
6. How did Peter and all other Apostles show that this authority was given to them?
7. Was the power of healing delegated to their successors or the power of the Word?
8. How does the key of the Word open and shut?

# The Keys of the Kingdom of Heaven
## (B) Christian Discipline

QUESTION 85 — *How is the kingdom of heaven shut and opened by Christian discipline?*

ANSWER — Thus: when according to the command of Christ, those who under the name of Christians, maintain doctrines or practices inconsistent therewith, and will not after having been often brotherly admonished, renounce their errors and wicked course of life, are complained of to the Church, or to those who are thereunto appointed by the Church: and if they despise their admonition, are by them forbidden the use of the sacraments; whereby they are excluded from the Christian Church, and by God himself from the kingdom of Christ; and when they promise and show real amendments, are again received as members of Christ and his Church.

●

Christian Discipline, the Achilles' heel of ecclesiastical supervision, is the second key of the kingdom of heaven. Instead of the Papal Ban, at which emperors trembled, marriages were not permitted and baptisms were illegal, the pendulum now swings in the opposite direction by not exercising any supervision in doctrine or daily practice.

During the Reformation, when Christ was again honored as the Head of the Church, the Papal Ban which was exclusively punitive, in the light of sacred Scripture was reformed into the key of Christian discipline, which was both punitive and corrective: the punitive power of excommunication and the corrective power of restitution. Thus we find in our Liturgy the office for church discipline consisting of two parts: 1. Excommunication. 2. Re-admission of the penitent.

While the key of the Preaching of the Gospel opens and shuts, the key of Christian Discipline shuts and opens.

*This key shuts.* If all Church members were perfect there would be no need of using this key. But inasmuch as both revelation and experience teach that in us, that is in our flesh, no good dwelleth, believers are subject to sinful thoughts and acts. Now, like in a home, minor offenses are not always punished, even though disapproved, so many transgressions are not always a subject for direct disciplinary action. Yet both communicant and baptized members who maintain doctrine or practice inconsistent with the Christian profession are subject to Christian discipline. Belgic Conf., Art. 32. Three stages in this discipline are noted. The first is a warning: "Go to thy brother" (Matt. 18:15). At times the brother objects and withdraws his membership by joining another church. Recognition of discipline of another church or denomination is not merely a matter of Christian ethics, but a pertinent requisite of loyalty to our own faith, which believes that this discipline is honored in heaven: then why not among brethren in the faith on earth? The second step is suspension from the privilege of Communion. After many pleadings, prayers and warnings, with permission of Classis, excommunication.

*This key opens.* The main object of discipline is to correct and to restore, and when repentance and confession result, the door is opened; it is still the day of grace! The erring brother may return and may be assured of being received with open arms into the Christian fellowship, and by the re-admission of the penitent the kingdom of heaven is opened by this key of Christian discipline.

The proper use of this key is essential to the spiritual welfare of the Church. Instead of revolting against it or escaping from it, believers should be weepingly thankful where the key of Christian discipline is rightly applied. No one then can complain: No man cared for my soul!

Great is the responsibility of the Church to exercise this key prayerfully and lovingly. Christian grace and humility are required to submit ourselves to the care and admonition of our spiritual leaders!

1. What is the second key of the kingdom of heaven?
2. Is Christian discipline both punitive and corrective?
3. What two corresponding forms are found in our Liturgy?
4. How does this second key shut?
5. What three stages are observed in using this key?
6. Is final excommunication within the jurisdiction of the local Church?
7. How does this key open?
8. Where did we promise to "submit to Christian care and admonition"?

# Our Service

## Sanctification and Good Works

QUESTION 86 — *Since then we are delivered from our misery, merely of grace, through Christ, without any merit of ours, why must we still do good works?*

ANSWER — Because Christ, having redeemed and delivered us by his blood, also renews us by his Holy Spirit, after his own image: that so we may testify, by the whole of our conduct, our gratitude to God for his blessings, and that he may be praised by us; also that every one may be assured in himself of his faith, by the fruits thereof; and that by our godly conversation, others may be gained to Christ.

QUESTION 87 — *Cannot they then be saved, who continuing in their wicked and ungrateful lives, are not converted to God?*

ANSWER — By no means; for the holy Scripture declares that no unchaste person, idolater, adulterer, thief, covetous man, drunkard, slanderer, robber, or any such like, shall inherit the kingdom of God.

●

Legalism — salvation through the works of the law — and Antinomianism — salvation without the works of the law — are the two rocks like Scylla and Charybdis upon which the frail boat of our faith may flounder. Expert seamanship is required to sail between these two extremes. Yes, we are saved without the law, and now being saved we obey the law out of gratitude.

In considering Justification and good works, the emphasis was on the insufficiency of good works. In considering Sanctification, the emphasis is on the necessity of good works.

If someone should object and say: First we are slaves of sin, cursed by the law; now we are slaves of Christ, bound to the law — so what is the gain? Then we note the distinction inasmuch as Christ has *renewed* us by his Holy Spirit, after his own image, so that the law is no hardship or slavery; it is the new fruit on the branch grafted in Christ. So the Psalmist speaks of the godly man: "His delight is in the law of the Lord" (Ps. 1:2). "O how love I thy law; it is my meditation all the day" (Ps. 119:97).

Thus there is still the necessity of good works in order that:

1. *God may be praised.* Being saved, we must show our gratitude to God for his blessings, so that he may be praised by us. We must do this "by the whole of our conduct," in thought, word and deed. The entire Christian life is a life of gratitude to God. The rule of that life is the law of God. When we learn to obey God's law because we love God, the giver of the law, then God indeed is praised. Thus we learn to live for the glory of God.

2. *That we may be assured of our faith.* It is explicitly stated here that we do not use good works as a measure to judge others. To the contrary: "that every one may be assured in himself." It is not meant for the condemnation of those who, according to our opinion, show little or no fruit, but it is meant for the self-examination of the believer concerning the fruitfulness of his own faith.

And even then, the believer may not make rash conclusions. Assurance of faith is primarily a work of the Holy Spirit; and, although our good works bear testimony to our faith, self-condemnation may be just as dangerous as self-praise. There are barren seasons in nature, and also in grace. A life time of service, rather than a single act, places weight in the scales. And even then God is judge.

3. *That others may be gained.* "That they may see your good works and glorify your Father who is in heaven" (Matt. 5:16). Good works exert a good influence, especially within the family circle, even though alone they do not gain others to Christ. But it follows that they who live in unrepented sin, idolaters, adulterers, thieves, and all others mentioned in Question 87 shall not inherit the Kingdom of God.

Question 91 tells us about the nature of good works:

a. *They must proceed from true faith.* That which is not of faith is sin in God's judgment. Be ye reconciled, is God's first demand. The unconverted may do civil good or moral good, but these are not good works in the sense in which we discuss it here.

b. *They must be done according to the law of God.* The burning of candles and prayers for the dead are not good works; they are "founded on the institutions of men."

c. *They must be done to his glory.* They must be done not for the praise of men or the glory of self, but wholeheartedly unto the Lord.

1. What is the relation between Justification and good works?
2. What is the relation between Sanctification and good works?
3. Explain dangers of legalism and Antinomianism.
4. Do Christians obey the law out of slavish fear?
5. What bearing has the Christian confession on the Christian behavior?
6. Give three reasons for the necessity of good works.
7. What is the three-fold test of good works?
8. What is the relation between assurance of faith and good works?

# True Conversion

QUESTION 88 — *Of how many parts doth the true conversion of man consist?*

ANSWER — Of two parts; of the mortification of the old, and of the quickening of the new man.

QUESTION 89 — *What is the mortification of the old man?*

ANSWER — It is a sincere sorrow of heart that we have provoked God by our sins, and more and more to hate and flee from them.

QUESTION 90 — *What is the quickening of the new man?*

ANSWER — It is a sincere joy of heart in God, through Christ, and with love and delight to live according to the will of God in all good works.

QUESTION 91 — *But what are good works?*

ANSWER — Only those which proceed from a true faith, are performed according to the law of God, and to his glory; and not such as are founded on our imaginations, or the institutions of men.

●

From the emphasis on *true* conversion, we infer that Biblical conversion is meant. A mere change of evil habits is not meant here. There is a reformation from flagrant crimes, and we speak of a converted drunkard. Some cite emotional experiences, a dream or a vision at death, or an accident as proof positive for their conversion. For good results in purer lives we are thankful, but true conversion requires:

1. *A twofold cause.* Both God and man are active in conversion. In its passive sense — "be converted" — the change

is attributed to God or divine agencies (Ps. 19:7. Matt. 18:3). When it appears in its active sense — "Repent" — it comes as a direct command to man. Conversion as a duty of man is mentioned 14 times as often as the statement that man is to be converted. (E. g., Acts 17:30.) God commandeth all men everywhere to repent.

Two words are used for this experience: one means a change of mind, and the other means a change of conduct. Both are used in one verse: "Repent ye therefore, and be converted" (Acts 13:19). But neither of these words agree with the Roman Catholic interpretation of penance.

2. *A twofold change.* First there is the mortification of the old self. Saul on the way to Damascus and the son refusing to labor in his father's vineyard followed the direction of their own mind and will. When we learn that our own will leads us in the wrong direction we hate and flee from evil; we stop and turn to God.

Then there is the quickening of the new man. Instead of doing our own will, we now ask: Lord, what wilt thou have me to do? When the prodigal son came to himself, he left the swine and said: I will arise and go to my father. A new joy comes into our heart, when we delight to do the will of God and to live according to his commandments.

This change is voluntary. A ship is "converted" by the helmsman; the horse is "converted," turned, by compulsion; ours is a willing change of mind. And that change of mind occurs again and again. Whenever we make decisions of a moral nature there must be a death of self-will, a mortification. That expression "mortification," with its sense of death, plainly indicates that this remains a difficult process. Yes, this change is voluntary, but God's grace is constantly needed in these decisions.

Conversion is also a definite act at a definite time, when first we surrender ourselves to the Lord. This experience varies with different individuals. One who has lived in sin for many years does not turn so readily from his evil: Jonah in the whale and Manasseh in prison were led through hard and difficult ways. Others who never lived in open rebellion and were trained in the way of the Lord, cannot point to extreme changes and experiences. Timothy knew the Word of the Lord from childhood days. Yet there must be a knowledge of sin, a repentance from sin, and faith in our Saviour.

Death-bed conversions like that of the Thief on the cross are possible but exceptional, and not advisable. "Today if you hear his voice, harden not your heart."

3. *A twofold result.* Good works are the result and the fruit of repentance. "Bring forth therefore fruits worthy of repentance" (Luke 3:8). Such good works proceed from a true faith, are performed according to the law of God and are done to his glory. The second result is growth in grace and in the knowledge of Christ, forgetting the things which are behind, and ever pressing onward and upward to the higher goal of spiritual and consecrated lives.

"Let us consider one another to provoke unto love and good works" (Heb. 10:24), and so make full proof of our true conversion.

1. What is the distinction between moral reformation and true conversion?
2. Give examples of true conversion from the Bible.
3. How does conversion differ from regeneration?
4. What is the difference between repentance and penance?
5. Name the twofold cause for conversion.
6. What is the necessary change in conversion?
7. What is the twofold result of conversion?
8. Do all Christians have the same manner of conversion?

# The Law of God

QUESTION 92 — *What is the law of God?*

ANSWER — God spake all these words saying, I am the Lord thy God, which have brought thee out of the land of Egypt, out of the house of bondage.

I. Thou shalt have no other gods before me.

II. Thou shalt not make unto thee any graven image, nor any likeness of anything that is in heaven above, or that is in the earth beneath, or that is in the water under the earth. Thou shalt not bow down thyself to them, nor serve them; for I, the Lord thy God, am a jealous God, visiting the iniquity of the fathers upon the children, unto the third and fourth generation of them that hate me, and showing mercy unto thousands of them that love me and keep my commandments.

III. Thou shalt not take the name of the Lord thy God in vain; for the Lord will not hold him guiltless that taketh his name in vain.

IV. Remember the sabbath day, to keep it holy. Six days shalt thou labour and do all thy work; but the seventh day is the sabbath of the Lord thy God; in it thou shalt not do any work, thou, nor thy son, nor thy daughter, thy man-servant, nor thy maid-servant, nor thy cattle, nor thy stranger that is within thy gates. For in six days the Lord made heaven and earth, the sea, and all that in them is, and rested the seventh day; wherefore the Lord blessed the sabbath day, and hallowed it.

V. Honour thy father and thy mother, that thy days may be long upon the land which the Lord thy God giveth thee.

VI. Thou shalt not kill.

VII. Thou shalt not commit adultery.

VIII. Thou shalt not steal.

IX. Thou shalt not bear false witness against thy neighbour.

X. Thou shalt not covet thy neighbour's house; thou shalt not covet thy neighbor's wife, nor his man-servant, nor his maid-servant, nor his ox, nor his ass, nor anything that is thy neighbour's.

QUESTION 93 — *How are these ten commands divided?*

ANSWER — Into two tables, the first of which teaches us how we must behave towards God; the second, what duties we owe to our neighbour.

●

Both previous subjects, "Sanctification and Good Works" and "Conversion," direct us to the Law of God expressed in the Ten Commandments.

The Civil Law is no longer binding since Israel as a nation ceased to exist.

The Ceremonial Law lost its power when realized in Christ.

But the Moral Law of the Ten Commandments was upheld by Christ (Matt. 22:37). Circumstances peculiarly divine prevailed when this law was given (Deut. 5:22). "These words the Lord spake with a great voice," and he preceded it with a solemn introduction (Ex. 20:1 and 2).

Acknowledged throughout the New Testament, this Old Testament moral law is in effect today although many who claim to live under grace deny this and now ignorantly sing: "Free from the law, oh, happy condition, Jesus has died and there is remission."

That is a good Gospel song in so far as it relates to our justification. But justification by faith leads to transformation of life, and there we learn to sing: "How gentle God's commands, how kind his precepts are."

Neglecting to read or to preach this law is to be delinquent in bringing the entire Gospel message. That blank page in the Bible between the Old and the New Testament does not mean that God in the Old Testament was severe in his legal demands, and that the New Testament brings a different revelation of love and grace. God is not changed, and the Bible is one complete revelation. The Law of God needs no amendments and has never been repealed. To be remiss in presenting the claims of this law in its interpretation of Christian life leads to carelessness weakness and sickness in the Church, and merits Jesus' warning: "Do the first works, or else I will remove thy candlestick out of its place" (Rev. 2:5). To utterly ignore or deny this law, brings us back to the vain search of the philosophers who tried to find the basis for moral behaviour in duty, reason, conscience or the sense of inward obligation.

The interpretation of the "ought," for some basis for ethical behaviour must be found. As Christians we are happy that this basis for Christian morality is found in the revealed will of God.

Law and grace are the two sides of the coin which is legal tender at the gate of Heaven.

There was grace in the O. T. when Noah preached 120 years before the flood came, when Jonah prophesied 40 days before impending destruction.

There is law in the N. T. when Jesus himself was born and died under the law, and when he taught: "Ye have heard that it was said by them of old time . . . but I say unto you. . ." "Do we then make void the law through faith?" wrote Paul. "God forbid; yea, we establish the law" (Rom. 3:31).

Thus the law still stands for the unconverted. It cannot make him virtuous, but it can discourage vice. By that law he is warned and restrained and that law like a schoolmaster can bring him to Christ.

Thus the law still stands for them that are saved by grace. In the light of that law we see our imperfections; we learn more and more to know our sinful nature and we pray for the grace of the Holy Spirit to strive for perfection. Its obedience now is not by reason of an outward force but by an inward compulsion. Jesus said: "I came to do the will of him that sent me" (John 6:37). Though imperfectly, we will try to do no less.

1. Is the Jewish civil law binding for us?
2. When was the ceremonial law ended?
3. Why is the moral law still in force?
4. What is the relation between grace and the law?
5. In what two Bible passages are the Ten Commandments recorded?
6. Was that law ever repealed or amended?
7. Explain the relation between law and grace in the O.T.
8. Explain the relation between grace and law in the N.T.

## God's Person

QUESTION 94 — *What doth God enjoin in the first command?*

ANSWER — That I, as sincerely as I desire the salvation of my own soul, avoid and flee from all idolatry, sorcery, soothsaying, superstition, invocation of saints, or any other creatures; and learn rightly to know the only true God; trust in him alone, with humility and patience submit to him; expect all good things from him only; love, fear and glorify him with my whole heart; so that I renounce and forsake all creatures, rather than commit even the least thing contrary to his will.

QUESTION 95 — *What is idolatry?*

ANSWER — Idolatry is, instead of or besides that one true God, who has manifested himself in his Word, to contrive or have any other object in which men place their trust.

●

Proclaimed in the days when polytheism was rampant, this First Commandment forms the foundation for the rest; it makes the others possible but also reasonable and understandable.

Moses learned it in the desert: "I am that I am." The Israelites held it as of supreme importance: "Hear ye, O Israel, the Lord thy God is one God."

Our Confession begins its first Article with the caption: *There is one only God,* a doctrine so essential for our generation which exalts the power of man's accomplishments, and lives as if there were no God with whom we have to do.

When we view what man's fertile imagination has furnished us in the world of religion; when we have seen all other gods and found no satisfaction, we too exclaim: "Whom have we in heaven but thee; and there is none upon earth besides thee."

*One divine essence* — our children should be taught this

vital truth first and foremost and repeatedly. When they learn that God fills the heavens; that in his creation he is everywhere, as we are everywhere in our body, then they readily reply to the question: "Why is there only one God?" "Because there is not room enough for two." And when grown up, our adults, who speak in terms of atomic power by which they can do what ten years ago they denied that God could do, need to hear of God's Sovereignty. They need to know that God occupies the highest place, that there is not room alongside him and surely nothing instead of him: "Thou shalt have no other gods *before me.*"

As surely as I desire the salvation of my soul I must avoid idolatry:

1. *In the physical realm.* This idolatry is called adultery in the Bible. Infidelity in secret is sinful, but to live in this sin openly, "before me," as the commandment reads, aggravates the evil: "Saying to a stock, Thou art my father; and to a stone; Thou hast brought me forth" (Jer. 2:27). The Asteroth, and Baal and Moloch; the worship of the sun, or fire, or the stars; all are evil. "The workman melteth a graven image, and the goldsmith spreadeth it over with gold"; and he that is poor "chooseth a tree that will not rot" (Is. 40:19f.). The polytheism of the heathen with impressive ceremonies of a bestial immorality; the Juggernaut; idolatry which we must flee and avoid; all are condemned by God.

2. *In the mental realm.* The word "idol" means that which is seen. And God is a spirit and as such invisible. But there are invisible idols too, those of the mind. There is a refined idolatry when in our mind we place other interests alongside of God or in the place of God. Sports and amusements are such idols to many, and the "stars" who furnish them are as gods to millions. Science and its pursuit occupies a large place in many minds, leaving God, who made the laws for science, out of consideration. The worship of wealth and of force by arms are other gods of our age. Self becomes a god in the worship of beauty and pride. Divided interests like those of the Samaritans who feared the Lord and served their own gods (II Kings 17:33) cause divided loyalty: God and Mammon, the church and the world. And more devastating than all, these ideas which man arrives at as exclusive creations of his mind; these ideologies, exalted in totalitarianism, nationalism, communism, are the soul-destroying idols of the modern man.

3. *In the spiritual realm.* The witch of Endor and Simon the sorcerer are Biblical illustrations. Our Communion liturgy warns against "enchanters, diviners, charmers, and those who confide in such enchantments." To seek or to believe them who claim to be able to foretell your future or your fortune, is to sin against this commandment. All superstitions of Friday, or 13, invocation of saints or other creatures, dreams and charms, games of luck, and many, many more instruments of the devil displace our trust in God's providence, and are various forms of idolatry.

Hence we must learn to know, trust, love and glorify God alone, committing "even the least thing" to his care. And there we all stand condemned.

1. Why is the First Commandment the foundation for the others?
2. What was Israel's confession concerning God's Person?
3. What has been the result of human imagination concerning the deity?
4. What is meant by "one divine essence"?
5. What are the evil results of idolatry?
6. What are physical images of God?
7. Name mental substitutes for God.
8. What is spiritism?

## God's Worship

QUESTION 96 — *What doth God require in the second command?*

ANSWER —That we in no wise represent God by images, nor worship him in any other way than he has commanded in his Word.

QUESTION 97 — *Are images then not at all to be made?*

ANSWER — God neither can, nor may be represented by any means: but as to creatures, though they may be represented, yet God forbids to make, or have any resemblance of them, either in order to worship them, or to serve God by them.

QUESTION 98 — *But may not images be tolerated in the churches, as books of the laity?*

ANSWER — No, for we must not pretend to be wiser than God, who will have his people taught, not by dumb images, but by the lively preaching of his Word.

●

On the basis of identity, Roman Catholics and Lutherans combine the first and second Commandment. Then, in order to maintain the number ten, they divide the last command into two.

However, there is a clear distinction: the first commandment deals with God's person, the second with God's worship. The first commandment teaches us that we must worship God; the second, how we must worship him.

True worship of God is considered:

1. *Negatively.* No image, symbol or similitude is to be made in order to worship them or serve God by them. Worship of God, like prayer, is the easiest and at the same time the most difficult exercise of the soul. Worship is the search of the soul for its counterpart. Since man lost the image in which God created him he found spiritual communion to be a perplexity, and substituted a physical representation. Witness the Israelites and the golden calf; Rachel's teraphim and the strange gods under the oak which was by Shechem. All creation is expressly set forth — "heaven above, or in the earth beneath, or in the water under the earth" — as not to be used in the worship of the Creator. And rightly so, for such worship dishonors God who is higher than any creature. Such worship is not true, for they are not true representations of God who is a spirit; such worship limits the conception of the worshiper, for that image cannot grow in his mind; and such worship is dangerous for it leads to idolatry, the sin of the First Commandment.

It is argued by those who have images in their worship of the true God that distinction is made in the kind of worship paid to the image; there is veneration, and the worship, or adoration, given to God alone. Perhaps some may keep that distinction in mind when they bow before an image of Mary or one of the saints. But for the laity, the child, the uninitiated, to all intents and purposes it is homage paid to images that are blind and dumb, and are not a help but a hindrance.

Nor are Roman Catholics or Lutherans the only transgressors of this commandment. Worshiping God in spirit and in truth is often obscured by a prominent or favored leader; ceremonies and forms may stand in the way; many who so rightly object to a crucifix, to nails of a saint, a thorn of the crown, Madonna, Pilate's staircase or the Pope's slipper, are erecting picture worship centers, or are confounding the stirring of the emotions by artistic and aesthetic performances for the spiritual joy of communion with God.

2. *Positively*. We must "worship God in no other way than he has commanded in his Word." Special punishment is meted out to the transgressor and special benefits are promised to those who obey this commandment. Man cannot rise higher than the object of his worship, and worshiping that which is lower than self ultimately brings the curse upon him and his posterity, for he becomes like that object in its moral and spiritual connections. Keeping the holy God before us we are drawn from things mundane to the very heart of God. Thus we read that after the golden calf was destroyed: "all the people rose up and worshipped, every man in his tent door" (Ex. 33:10). Saul learned that "to obey is better than sacrifice," and Jesus stated plainly that the true worshiper does not look to Gerizim or Jerusalem, but worships in spirit and in truth; and images are not spirit and they are not truth.

We are taught "by the lively preaching of the word." That word is living and he who brings it is living, spiritually. Even moving pictures or television cannot claim that.

The living Christ is the Living Word, and we come to God through him, who "is the image of the invisible God, the firstborn of every creature" (Col. 1:15). Rejecting him we are left to our own counterfeit devices of persons, places or things. Accept the image of God in Christ Jesus. He alone is the true and living Way.

1. Who combine the First and the Second Commandment?
2. How do you distinguish the First and the Second Commandment?
3. Give a definition of worship.
4. Why may we not use images in worship?
5. How do Roman Catholics distinguish the worship of images and the worship of God?
6. Why is worship so important?
7. What is Jesus' teaching in John 4:23?
8. Is there a place for television or moving pictures in worship?

# God's Name

QUESTION 99 — *What is required in the third command?*

ANSWER — That we, not only by cursing or perjury, but also by rash swearing, must not profane or abuse the name of God, nor by silence or connivance be partakers of these horrible sins in others; and briefly, that we use the holy name of God no otherwise than with fear and reverence; so that he may be rightly confessed and worshiped by us, and be glorified in all our words and works.

QUESTION 100 — *Is then the profaning of God's name, by swearing and cursing, so heinous a sin, that his wrath is kindled against those who do not endeavor, as much as in them lies, to prevent and forbid such cursing and swearing?*

ANSWER — It undoubtedly is; for there is no sin greater, or more provoking to God, than the profaning of his name; and therefore he has commanded this sin to be punished with death.

QUESTION 101 — *May we then swear religiously by the name of God?*

ANSWER — Yes, either when the magistrates demand it of the subjects, or when necessity requires us thereby to confirm fidelity and truth to the glory of God, and the safety of our neighbour; for such an oath is founded on God's Word, and therefore was justly used by the saints, both in the Old and New Testament.

QUESTION 102 — *May we also swear by saints or any other creatures?*

ANSWER — No, for a lawful oath is calling upon God, as the only one who knows the heart, that he will bear witness to the truth, and punish me if I swear falsely, which honour is due to no creature.

❂

This commandment finds its counterpart in the prayer Jesus taught his disciples: "Hallowed be thy name."

That name, rightly confessed, was Jesus' requirement for discipleship: "Whosoever therefore shall confess me before men, him will I confess before my Father who is in heaven" (Matt. 10:32).

To glorify that name in all our words and works becomes a Christian's lifetime task: "And whatsoever ye do in word or deed, do all in the name of the Lord Jesus" (Col. 3:17).

God's name, the revelation of his being, is of such supreme importance that even "highest angels speak not, e'er they veil their face." Hence we are warned at the risk of "bearing our iniquity" (Lev. 5:1) against:

*Irreverence.* God's name is constantly used in our praise and prayer and worship.

Little do we think that in formal prayer, in thoughtless praise, and in indifferent worship we are guilty of transgressing this commandment. God's name was considered so holy by the Jews that they paused in silence when reading the O. T. and found the word "Jehovah." They burned their old manuscripts containing this holy name, so that no unholy use could be made of the scroll. How careless have we become! "God bless you" may be a benediction, but it may at times be more than an empty phrase: the irreverent use of God's name.

*Profanity.* This is the use of the name of God without religious connotation in daily speech. That too is irreverent. But it is more: it is unprofitable, inexusable, unnecessary, profane. At times it contains or implies a wish or hope that the wrath of God may be meted out upon our fellowmen. Then truly we pray a devil's prayer. Verily, Isaiah's complaint, "I dwell in the midst of a people of unclean lips," (6:5) has its present-day application.

*Swearing* in the sense of cursing is profanity. The real sense of swearing is in connection with an oath, for the purpose of confirmation or witnessing.

Jesus warns against swearing as a daily occurrence for the purpose of confirmation or defending our own word or act. "Let your communication be Yea, yea; Nay, nay: whatsoever is more than these cometh of evil" (Matt. 5:37). We do not need to call upon God for every insignificant statement by way of confirmation, simply because the language of our own affirmation is already exhausted. Rash and foolish oaths are forbidden, as illustrated in the history of Jephthah, Herod and the forty Jews.

There is an appropriate use of the oath. An atheist cannot swear appropriately for he claims that he does not believe in God. A civic court cannot take such an oath, if the judge does not acknowledge God. The proper use of the oath in court is still a recognition of a power even beyond the Supreme Court of our land, and we rejoice in that usage as a tribute to God. The Bible gives illustrations of the use of oaths by God (Ps. 89:3), by Jesus (Matt. 26:64), by Paul (Rom. 1:9) that is permitted. Besides the requirement that the person using an oath must believe in God, it is also essential in the proper use of the oath (1) that the occasion is important. Marriage, the most sacred civil union, does not require it. Church membership, the most sacred spiritual union, does not call for it. Political organizations do not demand it. What can be so important, then? The appearance before a tribunal when we witness, and life or death may depend on it, may be such. (2) The administration must be lawful. Since all government is under God, a civil court or a Church court may administer an oath, but no oath is required of a minor even then. (3) The contents must be known. We are careful with our name; with one stroke of the pen we can sign away our property. How careful we ought to be with God's name, when we can swear away his blessing and invoke his curse (Lev. 5:4)!

*Perjury* is a false statement under oath which the court of the land severely punishes. How much more sinful it must be in the eyes of God!

Our prayer should be: "Unite my heart to fear thy name" (Ps. 86:11).

1. What is the N. T. counterpart of this Commandment?
2. Why is confession of Christ's name a condition of discipleship?
3. How is God's name glorified?
4. What are the dangers of irreverence in using God's name?
5. Why is profanity such a great evil?
6. Are oaths permissible?
7. What are the three requirements for an oath?
8. What is meant by perjury?

## God's Day

QUESTION 103 — *What doth God require in the fourth command?*

ANSWER — First, that the ministry of the Gospel and the schools be maintained; and that I, especially on the Sabbath, that is, on the day of rest, diligently frequent the Church of God, to hear his Word, to use the sacraments, publicly to call upon the Lord, and contribute to the relief of the poor, as becomes a Christian; secondly, that all the days of my life I cease from my evil works, and yield myself to the Lord, to work by his Holy Spirit in me; and thus begin in this life the eternal Sabbath.

●

Our sense of proportion receives a severe jolt, when we note four questions were devoted to God's name and here only one to

God's day. That impact is not cushioned by the abrupt interpretation in the answer given. In vain we look for "do's and don't's," or for a milder explanation of Sabbath observance according to the wish of those who do not find the literal reproduction of this commandment in the N. T. No change of the Sabbath is referred to, in commemoration of Jesus' resurrection, or any defense against those who still observe the seventh day, and who identify the Lord's Day with the Sign of the Beast.

None of these and other controversies face us here. But painted brightly against the background of God's creative act, the believer, "as becomes a Christian," is pictured doing the Lord's work on the Sabbath; applying the spirit of that work in his everyday life; and beginning "in this life the eternal Sabbath." Hence for the Christian the Lord's Day is:

1. *An imitation* of God's rest from creation. He rested the seventh day; he blessed it, and hallowed it. Antedating Sinai, this commandment was observed at the distribution of manna (Ex. 16:23). It was forgotten or neglected in Egypt. Hence the ancient precept was recalled by beginning: "Remember." It was a divine law by way of example and command. No people on their own impulse introduced it. The Chinese civilization had no Sabbath. French atheists invented a tenth day interim and failed. But wherever Christianity gains ground, the banner of the Sabbath becomes a sign of faith in God's creative act and his rest on the seventh day (Gen. 2:3).

2. *An application* of spiritual activities. God rested, but not in idleness. Jesus said: "My Father worketh hitherto, and I work" (John 5:17). While the commandment negatively states: "in it thou shalt do no manner of work," the answer plunges us positively into works permissible and compulsory: the ministry of the Gospel, which covers a large territory — the whole wide world; the schools for training for Christian life and service; Church attendance for worship; hearing the Word for upbuilding in the faith; using the sacraments publicly as a testimony; prayer and contribution for the poor: yes, truly, all for the good of self and others, the Sabbath was made for man. Mark 2:27.

What a calamity, what a loss when the Sabbath is forgotten and none of these acts prevail! See heathen nations! And what a benediction if believers can be, like John, in the Spirit on the Lord's day (Rev. 1:10; Isaiah 58:23 and 24).

3. *A preparation* for all the days of our life and for eternity.

Yielding ourselves unto the Lord, his Holy Spirit continues to work in us during the remaining days of the week to enable us to cease from evil works and to honor God in our Christian life. How true that is in the New Testament dispensation! In the Old Testament there were six days of work followed by the day of rest, bringing the fruit of works to the Lord. Our worship on the first day emphasizes our beginning with grace which is followed by six days of work in the strength of that grace. By that grace the entire week is hallowed and sanctified.

That preparation looks beyond time when through the influence of the Lord's Day we begin in this life the eternal Sabbath. Yes, there is a rest remaining for the people of God, but not a rest of idleness any more than here. A favorite description of Heaven is, "And his servants shall serve him" (Rev. 22:3).

Forgetting the Lord's Day is forgetting the Lord; keep the world out; keep work down; keep the Spirit in; this is a good way of keeping the Sabbath.

A week without a Sabbath is like a summer without sun, like a flower without scent or color. The Lord's Day is our Pisgah from which we view the Promised Land. It is an Elim for the pilgrim. It is an emblem of life eternal.

1. Why is the Sabbath called the Lord's Day?
2. Why is not the Fourth Commandment the basis for the Lord's Day?
3. When was the Sabbath observed before the Law was given?
4. How is rest interpreted?
5. What activities are mentioned?
6. How is the Sabbath a blessing for man?
7. Is Heaven a place of service?
8. For what is the Lord's Day a preparation?

# God's Rulers

QUESTION 104 — *What doth God require in the fifth command?*

ANSWER — That I show all honor, love and fidelity to my father and mother, and all in authority over me, and submit myself to their good instruction and correction, with due obedience; and also patiently bear with their weaknesses and infirmities, since it pleases God to govern us by their hand.

●

"Disobedient to parents" (II Tim. 3:2) is mentioned as one of the signs of the last days and one of the causes of perilous times. Written so long ago, these words still find their application today in our homes. And in a wider sense, "all authority" by which it pleases God to govern us, is covered by this commandment. Hence we learn that parental esteem is the basis of:

1. *The Christian home.* The importance of this commandment is seen in its position in the decalogue: immediately after the relationship with God follows our relationship with our parents, both father and mother. We owe our parents our *honor,* as Joseph honored his shepherd father before the king. Even if obedience is not stated, honor expresses recognition of dignity and worth, and therefore requires obedience (Eph. 6:2). Obedience could be slavish, out of fear for punishment, or with resentment. Even when our parents are no longer with us, and obedience is out of the question, we can still honor them. We owe our parents our *love.* A child can never repay its mother's sacrifice and its father's care. We owe our parents our *fidelity.* Jesus was subject unto his parents. He remembered his mother in the midst of his own agony. This includes patience in their weaknesses and assistance in their infirmities of age or poverty, because it pleased God that they should be our parents, and we are to be true to them.

2. *The Christian Church.* Inasmuch as the home is the foundation for the Church, obedience to parents is the first step in obedience to God. They who never learned obedience to their earthly father, have little conception of obedience to God who is their heavenly Father. We bestow no favor upon our children by letting them grow up without respect, reverence, or obedience. The result will be indifference and disobedience to the laws of God. There are authorities which God has placed in the Church. Disobedience to these officers is a transgression against this commandment, and so against God. Divisions of the body of Christ, schisms because of some dissatisfaction or disagreement, are serious sins. To be sure, that obedience too is "in the Lord," hence Peter and John were disobedient to authorities who acted contrary to the will of God (Acts 4:19). But most cases of separation cannot claim this reason.

3. *The Christian State.* "Servants, be obedient to them that are your masters according to the flesh" (Eph. 6:5). The rules of that obedience are plainly set forth in the following verses. And those in authority have similar obligations: "And ye masters, do the same things unto them." Sacredness of contract between employer and employee refers to honesty in payment and honesty of time and labor given.

And we think of our obedience to local, state and national laws and authorities. The position of Christians in a state hostile to our Christ; revolutions in the past and our own war for Independence are instances in which a Christian must choose between the authority of the State or the authority of God. Even in a Christian state we have at times to "bear with their weaknesses and infirmities."

This is the first commandment with a promise. Ruth is a shining example, and Absalom and the sons of Eli are stern warnings from the Holy Book. Disobedience to parents leads to bad habits and evil company, and the wages of sin is death. Perhaps the promise is of a wider interpretation for generations and nations.

1. Does the place of the Fifth Commandment indicate its importance?
2. Why are "honor, love and fidelity" mentioned instead of obedience?
3. Who are in authority over us?
4. Are our rulers under the authority of God?
5. Are evil rulers under God's authority? John 19:11.
6. Is parental authority the basis for authority toward God, the Church, the State?
7. How does this commandment apply to employer and employee?
8. When is resistance against authority permissible?

## The Sanctity of Life

QUESTION 105 — *What doth God require in the sixth command?*

ANSWER — That neither in thoughts, nor words, nor gestures, much less in deeds, I dishonor, hate, wound, or kill my neighbor, by myself or by another; but that I lay aside all desire of revenge; also, that I hurt not myself, nor wilfully expose myself to any danger; wherefore also the magistrate is armed with the sword to prevent murder.

QUESTION 106 — *But this command seems only to speak of murder?*

ANSWER — In forbidding murder, God teaches us that he abhors the causes thereof; such as envy, hatred, anger, and desire of revenge; and that he accounts all these as murder.

QUESTION 107 — *But is it enough that we do not kill any man in the manner mentioned above?*

ANSWER — No; for when God forbids envy, hatred and anger, he commands us to love our neighbour as ourselves; to show patience, peace, meekness, mercy, and all kindness, towards him; and prevent his hurt as much as in us lies; and that we do good even to our enemies.

Out of the slimy depths of man's inhumanity to man we have come face to face with these monsters of hate and revenge, pride and envy. It is not a pleasant task to drag them from their dark caverns to view them in the light of the revealed Word of God. But only thus we learn that man's brutal power to take human life, from Cain's fratricide to the Jewish massacres, world wars, political purges and atomic destructions, are still in sharp contrast with the divine law to maintain the sanctity of human life, so simply stated: Thou shalt not kill.

1. *The literal interpretation.* The Bible teaches us the frailty of human life and pictures it as a shadow and a vapor, a flower of the. field and a weaver's shuttle; but this does not invalidate the sanctity of human life. We are warned against:

*Homicide,* as accidental manslaughter. Even though the accident is not immediately fatal, there still is the period of one year and one day in which it comes under the heading of homicide. During the days of the blood avenger, the Cities of Refuge provided a stay of retribution (Deut. 19).

Homicide as premeditated manslaughter is murder.

Homicide as participated manslaughter may be of lesser degree in man's judgment, but the history of David and Uriah gives us the judgment of God.

*Suicide,* like that of Saul who died in his sin, and Judas who went his own way, whether by euthanasia or wilful exposure to danger, is here condemned. Death does not end all, nor does it furnish escape from responsibility.

Capital punishment may here be debated. Fear of wrong judgment; opportunity for conversion are held as arguments against the death penalty. But Jesus acknowledged Pilate's right to take life as given from above (John 19:11). War and the claims of religious objectors may here be considered: the Catechism quotes Rom. 13:4 concerning rulers: "He beareth not the sword in vain."

2. *Spiritual interpretation.* Jesus taught us that not only the poisonous fruit but that also the root of bitterness must be eradicated (Matt. 6:22). The anger of Cain, the spirit of vengeance of Simeon and Levi (Gen. 34), the envy of Joseph's brethren; the hate of the Pharisees against Jesus, were motives in their evil deeds which God accounts as murder. Of these evil motives in the human heart it may well be said: their name is legion. Uncontrolled desires lead to alcoholism and intemperance in eating and drinking; unfair profit motives lead to unsanitary food products; the love of

money makes poison peddlers of habit-forming drugs; even our "thoughts, words and gestures" as expressions of hate are forbidden.

3. *A positive interpretation.* That part of the summary of the law whereby we are told to love our neighbor as ourselves, applies here. When by the grace of God the Holy Spirit renews a right spirit within us, then we can show patience, peace, meekness, mercy and all kindness toward others. We learn to do good and to pray even for our enemies. We will not try to hurt but prevent possible harm: Deut. 22:8.

Am I my brother's keeper? Of course you are, since Christ gave his life for you and for him. Then when we compare our transactions with our fellowmen in the light of the cross, a blush of self-condemnation floods our soul, when again we hear or read this commandment.

1. Why do we speak of the sanctity of human life?
2. What was the purpose of the Cities of Refuge in the O. T.?
3. What is homicide?
4. Is capital punishment allowed?
5. Is war against the teaching of this commandment?
6. How do uncontrolled desires lead to the transgression of this commandment?
7. What is the positive interpretation of this commandment?
8. How did Jesus enlarge this commandment? Matt. 5:22.

# Purity of Life

QUESTION 108 — *What doth the seventh command teach us?*

ANSWER — That all uncleanness is accursed of God, and that, therefore, we must, with all our hearts, detest the same, and live chastely and temperately, whether in holy wedlock, or in a single life.

QUESTION 109 — *Doth God forbid in this command, only adultery, and such like gross sins?*

ANSWER — Since both our body and soul are temples of the Holy Ghost, he commands us to preserve them pure and holy; therefore he forbids all unchaste actions, gestures, words, thoughts, desires and whatever can entice men thereto.

●

The fifth commandment deals with the origin of life, the sixth with the sanctity of life, and this commandment deals with the purity of life, "whether in holy wedlock or in single life."

Family life in its state of monogamy, is a product of the

teaching of the Bible. There we also learn that the most sacred relationship between Christ and the believer—Christ and the Bride—is compared to the most sacred relationship in human life—husband and wife. Hence the breaking or the defiling of this relationship is compared to the breaking or defiling of the marriage vow, expressed in the word adultery. We learn that:

1. *Marriage* is a sacred institution and must not be defiled or dissolved.

Marriage is honorable in all (Heb. 13:3), and forbidding to marry is described as a departure from the faith (I Tim. 4:3). Regarding divorce, the question of the Pharisees in Jesus' time is still up-to-date. And Jesus' answer still stands, disputed, doubted and denied but still unsurpassed. Jesus' statement about leaving father and mother to cleave to his wife (Matt. 19:5), was quoted from the time when there was neither father nor mother to leave (Gen. 2:24). "And they shall be one flesh," one personality which admits of no separation. Free love, socialization of women, trial marriages, are all under condemnation.

Blood marriage, as unlawful and detailed in Lev. 18, may not seem improper for us, but close family relationship in marriage still leads to sterility and insanity. Mixed marriages were strictly forbidden between Israelites and heathen nations: remember Abraham's concern for Isaac. People of different creed and breed may contract marriage in our American melting pot, but often all religion is melted out. Protestants marrying Catholics, atheists, or just non-believers have little hope for a successful married life.

Polygamy is a federal offense, and had to be removed in Utah before it could join the Union. Polygamy is mentioned in the Bible, but never with God's approval. Concubinage is unlawful. Secret marriage is a dangerous procedure for the sake of placing temptations in the path of others and because marriage is a public commitment. Adultery in wedlock is the one Biblical ground for divorce.

2. *Personal Life* is a sacred gift and we must glorify God in our body (I Cor. 6:20).

Lust, lasciviousness, concupiscence, evil passions and uncontrolled desires and sinful thoughts must be counteracted by being filled with the Spirit of God. Paul's advice to Timothy contains much good (I Tim. 5:22). "If any man defile the temple of God, him shall God destroy" (I Cor. 3:17). "Know ye not that your body is the temple of the Holy Ghost" (I Cor. 6:19)? Early parental training is mandatory. Overcoming evil with good is still excellent Biblical precept.

3. *Social Life* is of divine origin and must be safeguarded. We are not created without inter-relationship: we are not grains of sand. Even heathen have their taboos. Christianity teaches the highest degree of morality and mutual responsibility, something not observed in our social life. Foul speech in the mouth of older folks poisons many a child's mind. Dirty anecdotes have no place in decent conversation. The road of evil company and smutty sheets of literature, the road of the public dance and indecent dress oppose purity in our social life. Spring cleaning should mean more than painting homes and cleaning dirty alleys. Governmental authorities seem to deal more with the evil consequences than with preventive causes of public immorality. Lot's experience and Dinah's defilement are not antiquated illustrations of the warning in Deut. 23:17.

As we firmly believe that Christ the heavenly Bridegroom shall present us without spot or wrinkle before the Father, may we so live together practicing and defending purity in married or in single life.

1. To what is the relationship between husband and wife compared?
2. Is monogamy a universal institution?
3. What is blood marriage?
4. What are results of mixed marriages?
5. How can we promote personal purity?
6. Should parents supervise their children's reading material?
7. Do our authorities censor movies, television?
8. How did Jesus apply this commandment?

# Our Property

QUESTION 110 — *What doth God forbid in the eighth command?*

ANSWER — God forbids not only thefts, and robberies, which are punishable by the magistrate, but he comprehends under the name of theft all wicked tricks and devices, whereby we design to appropriate to ourselves the goods which belong to our neighbor, whether it be by force, or under the appearance of right, as by unjust weights, ells, measures, fraudulent merchandise, false coins, usury, or by any other way forbidden by God; as also all covetousness, all abuse and waste of his gifts.

QUESTION 111 — *But what doth God require in this command?*

ANSWER — That I promote the advantage of my neighbour in every instance I can or may; and deal with him as I desire to be dealt with by others; further also, that I faithfully labour, so that I may be able to relieve the needy.

●

In no sphere of human activities is conscience so dull and deficient as in the application of this commandment. Rachel stole her father's household gods with no more pangs of conscience than Jacob obtained his birthright under false pretense. When Malachi complains about robbing God, only few are disturbed at this possibility. Achan's wedge of gold and Judas' bag teach us that even in the army of the Lord and among the disciples of Christ the voice of conscience was not heard in a whisper.

But one should hear it. Conscience is sometimes silenced by perverted interpretations of stealing under the fancy names of graft, bribery, profiteering which are considered too common to raise objection. Or, stealing comes in forms which evil practices no longer pronounce to be stealing, such as raffles, gambling or lotteries.

And when we are here taught that covetousness and the waste of God's gifts are comprehended under the name of theft, many Christian consciences need to be trained by this divine law. This can be done by considering:

1. *What God Forbids.* Property rights are upheld in the Bible and recognized by the State. Thefts and robberies are thus punished by the magistrates, as well as condemned by God. Then there is a religious no-man's-land, where the State has no jurisdiction but where God, who looks upon the intents of the heart, speaks to us about the moral obligations of the "ought." Misrepresentation of goods, devaluation of quality under a known trade name, wicked tricks and devices such as gambling, lotteries, games of cards or dice, are designed to appropriate to ourselves the goods which belong to our neighbor and the man with a Christian conscience should refrain.

Honest hours for fair wages are obligations of the laboring man, and stealing five or ten minutes is stealing. In business just weights and measures are required: divers weights are an abomination unto the Lord (Prov. 20:23).

2. *Why God Forbids It.* Stealing is against the revealed

will of God, let that suffice. No child should be trained to refrain from stealing for fear that theft will be discovered. He should be trained to know that God does not want him to steal.

And should we be asked why God forbids, the Bible directs us to the fact that God is the absolute and ultimate owner of all: "the earth is the Lord's and the fulness thereof" (Ps. 24). "For every beast of the forest is mine, and the cattle upon a thousand hills" (Ps. 50:10). "The silver is mine, and the gold is mine, saith the Lord of hosts" (Hag. 2:8). We are stewards and co-laborers. Taking goods from one another is stealing from God. He gives each according to his ability. "The Lord maketh poor, and maketh rich" (I Sam. 2:7). Attempts to remove stealing by removing poverty; the equality of socialism or compulsory, athe-istic communism do not reckon with this divine law. And poverty is by no means the one reason for stealing: rich people steal and often get away with it.

3. *What God Commands.* The golden rule and the sum-mary of the law teach us God's command in a positive way. More specifically Question 111 states that I must promote the ad-vantage of my neighbor in every instance I can, or may. We should labor faithfully so that we may share with others. Chris-tian benevolence should not be endangered by a paternalistic state. We still have the poor to whom the Gospel must be preached. Crop curtailment is no help to starving millions elsewhere. Our abun-dance is our opportunity, not our curse.

Our treasure is in Heaven, but our responsibility for our earthly treasure is here. "I was an hungred, and ye gave me meat." When Zacchaeus said: "Lord, the half of my goods I give to the poor, and what I have taken I restore fourfold," Jesus approved: "This day is salvation come to this house." So be it to us.

1. Who is the absolute owner of all things?
2. Does the Bible uphold personal property rights?
3. Are small thefts sinful?
4. What other forms of transgression does this commandment deal with?
5. Do we warn against theft because it will be found out?
6. Is "crime does not pay" a sufficient warning?
7. What is Christian stewardship?
8. What is the positive interpretation of this commandment?

# Our Words

QUESTION 112 — *What is required in the ninth command?*

ANSWER — That I bear false witness against no man; nor falsify any man's words; that I be no backbiter, nor slanderer; that I do not judge, or join in condemning any man rashly, or unheard; but that I avoid all sorts of lies and deceit, as the proper works of the devil, unless I would bring down upon me the heavy wrath of God; likewise that in judgment and all other dealings I love the truth, speak it uprightly and confess it; also that I defend and promote, as much as I am able, the honour and good character of my neighbour.

●

Words may be cheap, but they can cost us plenty. Every word we speak is a choice between the great antithesis of truth and lie. The devil, diabolus, the false accuser, is the father of lies, and spoke the first lie to Eve. We speak in the name of and under the tutelage of Christ, who said: I am the truth.

This commandment follows and is closely connected with the previous law of stealing. There it was my neighbor's possessions. Here it is my neighbor's name and honor. In comparison the ninth commandment points to a far more serious crime than stealing goods. Who steals my purse, steals trash; but our good name is all some of us have, and all of us should treasure it above gold.

The spoken word is beyond recall; it flies like an arrow to its mark. Woe unto thee if it kills or wounds where no hurt was deserved. "Lying lips are an abomination to the Lord" (Prov. 12:22). "Lie not one to another" (Col. 13:9). God forbids:

1. *False Witness.* We meet our neighbors in our private life and our family circle. Deliberate prevarication in misrepresenting the truth is a great evil. There is a form of childish exaggeration which is just a product of immature imagination and at times we can smile at that. But a deliberate lie breaks the tie of friendship: such persons are no longer dependable. Half a truth can be a whole lie. Evil news when true becomes a source of gossip. Evil words when not true are slander and can be turned against the speaker as libel. All we know need not be told, whether good or evil; "A fool layeth open his folly" (Prov. 13:16). White lies and speaking with mental reservation or speaking lies for a good cause may be Jesuitism but it is adulterated Christianity. Silence can be a lie. Irony is not meant as a lie, as

when Elijah was speaking to the priests of Baal (I Kings 18:27), but for the uninitiated, it remains a sharp tool that can hurt both speaker and hearer. False or premature judgment of the actions of others leads to the transgression of this commandment. All these bring down upon the transgressor "the heavy wrath of God."

We meet our neighbors in social or in public life, in politics, in business, in school, in church. Absalom pretended kindness to gain followers. The Gibeonites acted out the lie with their worn-out garments. Ananias lied against the Holy Spirit. They who serve the public are subject to all kinds of falsifications. The President of our nation is quoted partially with wrong emphasis or intonation. The good name of our leaders in Church and State is assailed: in the Church most people do not read Ps. 105:15, and in the State few care to run for office. These are evils under the sun which are detrimental to our people and are punished by God.

Sometimes, not often, we meet our neighbors in court. To refuse to testify when witnesses are needed and when we can witness can be of infinite harm to the accused. It does not often happen to the average person that he is placed under oath in a court to speak the truth, the whole truth and nothing but the truth. A lie under oath is perjury, and was discussed under the third commandment. I Kings 21:13 tells of Jezebel's false witnesses against Naboth. There were also false witnesses against Christ.

Always we meet our neighbors, seen or unseen, in our religious life. Acts 1:8, "ye shall be witnesses unto me," places the issue squarely before us. God demands:

2. *Good Witness.* Our confession of faith is a good witness to our faith in Christ who is the truth. Spreading our religion requires that we are "not ashamed of the testimony of our Lord" (II Tim. 1:8). May our prayer be, "Deliver my soul, O Lord, from lying lips" (Ps. 120:2).

1. What do we owe to our neighbor's name and honor?
2. What is gossip? slander?
3. When is silence a lie?
4. Can we act a lie?
5. What is false witness under oath?
6. Can unwillingness to witness be harmful?
7. What does a good witness testify?
8. How do we witness in regard to our faith?

# Our Thoughts

QUESTION 113 — *What doth the tenth commandment require of us?*

ANSWER — That even the smallest inclination or thought, contrary to any of God's commands, never rise in our hearts; but that at all times we hate all sin with our whole hearts, and delight in all righteousness.

⬤

There is no civil law against the transgressor of this commandment. No one ever was tried in the courts of the land because he was covetous. Hence many think that the last commandment is the least. Even Paul declared that he had not known lust to be sin, except the law had said: "Thou shalt not covet" (Rom. 7:7).

The tenth commandment is by no means the least of the commandments. It warrants the interpretation of all the others, not only literally but spiritually; for all commandments and their transgressions find their roots in our thoughts.

*Covetousness* is defined as inordinate, uncontrolled, illegitimate desire for what is not ours, which makes for unhappiness when it is not obtained, which we try to get by means fair or foul.

A single wish is not covetousness. Ambition and a desire to excel in business or in a game is not evil. A pupil in school without ambition will never learn. Nor is a desire for advancement wrong. If for good reason a recognition comes to us in Church or State and we are placed in a responsible position above others, we may accept; but if it does not come to us, we are to abide by the will of God.

Covetousness leads to dissatisfaction and selfishness which are the roots of every crime mentioned in the decalogue. It led to disobedience in our first parents; to the stealing of Achan, to the rebellion of Absalom, to the betrayal of Christ; to the loss of a soul (Luke 12:15, 20).

Covetousness makes for unhappiness in people who want to compete with others above their station. It is one of the sins of our age, evident in the coveting of the servant to be the master, and of the rich to become richer. It leads to monopoly in restraint of trade, and world cartels, a source of wars.

Extravagance in display which few can afford but many want lights the spark of desire which bursts into uncontrollable flames of evil deeds to get what is wanted. Like the grave it never says: enough. In our national life it makes for manifold difficulties, to strikes and lock-outs when people forget the Word of God that a man's life consisteth not in the abundance of things which he possesseth. Even if the goal is obtained there is no satisfaction, and there is no happiness.

Positively this commandment requires moral contentment which through the grace of God can come to our hearts. Paul had learned in whatsoever state he was, therewith to be content. "Godliness with contentment is great gain." We might learn this in the school of life, but life is too short to learn by experiences and the tuition is too high. Trusting in God's providence, not being indifferent in regard to progress but with humble prayer and earnest effort, we can accept what God gives. This commandment requires that we hate all sin, but also that we delight in all righteousness. There are desires of the heart, so sincere, and so ambitious, that the Bible uses the expression: "Covet earnestly the best gifts" (I Cor. 12:31), and "Covet to prophesy" (I Cor. 14:39). Paul states that his heart's desire and prayer to God for Israel is that they might be saved. If we coveted salvation for our child as much as we covet success in the world; if we were as covetous for the riches of God as for stocks and bonds; if we were as anxious to be dressed in the righteousness of Christ as our body to be adorned with silks and satins; if we worked as hard for divine approval as for the world's approbation, life would have a larger meaning and a lasting joy.

The tenth commandment is like the rudder: it steers the whole ship of the decalogue.

1. Is covetousness a civil offense?
2. What is the relation of this commandment to the other nine?
3. Define covetousness.
4. Distinguish covetousness from ambition.
5. What may covetousness lead to?
6. What promotes covetousness?
7. What is the positive interpretation of this commandment?
8. May we covet good gifts?

# The Believer and the Law

QUESTION 114 — *But can those who are converted to God, perfectly keep these commands?*

ANSWER — No; but even the holiest men, while in this life, have only small beginnings of this obedience; yet so, that with a sincere resolution, they begin to live not only according to some, but all the commands of God.

QUESTION 115 — *Why will God then have the ten commands so strictly preached since no man in this life can keep them?*

ANSWER — First, that all our life time, we may learn more and more to know our sinful nature, and thus become the more earnest in seeking the remission of sin, and righteousness in Christ; likewise, that we constantly endeavor and pray to God for the grace of the Holy Spirit; that we may become more and more conformable to the image of God, till we arrive at the perfection proposed to us, in a life to come.

●

Whence knowest thou thy misery? Out of the law of God. At the very beginning of the Catechism that statement led us to the Mediator, our Lord Jesus Christ who fulfilled the law for us. Now that we are the Lord's, there still is the question concerning the law. In fact, two questions are considered:

1. *Can the believer keep the law perfectly?* The answer is: *No.* The unbeliever cannot keep the law: "the carnal mind is not subject to the law of God, neither indeed can be" (Rom. 8:7). They think and say they do: "All these have I kept from my youth up" (Luke 18:21), but they forget the positive and the spiritual interpretation of the law. The believer cannot keep the law perfectly, for even the holiest of men is not perfect. No one has ever reached perfection in the arts, or claimed perfection in knowledge: how can we claim it then in religion?

In opposition to those who claim that some have more good works than they need, as Roman Catholicism teaches, and in opposition to *perfectionists* who claim to be perfect, the Bible teaches us that we have only small beginnings of this obedience. None of the Bible saints in the Old or New Testament claimed perfection. Only Christ said: "Who of you convinces me of sin?"

Nevertheless with a sincere resolution the believer begins to live according to all the commandments of God. "For I delight in the law of God after the inward man" (Rom. 7:22). Paul counted not himself to have apprehended, but he had an earnest desire: "I press toward the mark for the prize of the high calling of God in Christ Jesus" (Phil. 3:14).

2. *Does the believer need the law?* The answer is: *Yes.* The unbeliever needs the law. For him it may be a deterrent principle. It may become a schoolmaster to bring him to Christ.

The believer, like the Antinomians, might think that since Christ fulfilled the law, the law no longer is intended for him. Yes, some may commit sin, in order that grace may abound. But Paul states: "God forbid, how shall we, that are dead to sin, live any longer therein" (Rom. 6:2)? Yes, we need the reading of the law in the Church; the preaching of the law for the believer and the self-examination which the law furnishes. The preaching of the law will bring the believer to a deeper knowledge of his sinful nature. That knowledge was first needed in order that through the law there might come a knowledge of sin which brought him to Christ. Now that he is in Christ, the more he realizes the sinfulness of his nature, the more he will seek remission of sin and the righteousness of Christ. His spiritual conception is more exacting. He obeys the law which demands perfection, and he sees his own imperfection better than ever. Now he knows he needs Christ for his pardon but also for his righteousness every day of his life. It brings him to a deeper conviction that, for him, all is grace.

Furthermore the believer needs the law for his constant endeavor to become perfect. That is a life-long process: "until we arrive at the perfection proposed to us, in a life to come." Meanwhile with prayer to God for the grace of the Holy Spirit there is a constant endeavor to become more and more conformable to the image of God, lost through sin, restored by grace, and perfected in Heaven. It becomes a law for our sanctification which we will need till the time of our holiness.

1. Having learned the positive interpretation of the commandments, can we say that we keep the law?
2. Can we keep the law in its spiritual interpretation?
3. What do Roman Catholics teach about good works?
4. What is perfectionism?
5. What does the law do for the believer?
6. What do Antinomians teach about the law?
7. Is the teaching of the law still necessary?
8. What is the relation between sanctification and the law?

# Our Need of Prayer

QUESTION 116 — *Why is prayer necessary for Christians?*

ANSWER — Because it is the chief part of thankfulness which God requires of us: and also, because God will give his grace and Holy Spirit to those only who with sincere desires continually ask them of him, and are thankful for them.

●

Having studied the requirements of the law in its evangelical setting, it may appear strange that, following this, prayer is called "that chief part of thankfulness which God requires of us."

By way of explanation it should be pointed out that obedience to the law of God as an act of gratitude finds its root in communion with God, and this communion is most readily conceived of as prayer. For in prayer the soul reaches up to the eternal and the invisible, far above self, the world and its trials and troubles. Here the Christian waits upon the Lord.

No wonder, then, that the language of Canaan is adorned with glorious descriptions — which are not necessarily theological definitions — of prayer. Prayer is called the link between heaven and earth. Prayer is speaking to God. Prayer is the breath of the soul. Prayer is the Christian's native air. Prayer is the avenue of the Spirit to the soul. Prayer is the soul's sincere desire. Prayer is the optic nerve of the soul. Prayer is the simplest form of speech — and the sublimest strains that reach the majesty on high. Prayer is a holy art.

Then let the scoffer argue that prayer is unnecessary, superfluous, superstitious, auto-suggestive, unreasonable. Such mockery is robbing the cripple of his crutches; it is clipping the eagle of his wings, for prayer is inherently and universally an expression of human need. It is not even a unique feature of the Christian religion. All men pray at some time in their lives.

But a Christian — is it necessary for him too? A Christian believes in a divine Being who is omniscient and a heavenly Father who is benevolent; he believes in God's sovereignty and immutability — then why should he pray?

1. *Because God requires it.* This requirement surpasses the common explanation of literal commandments to pray so frequently found in the Scriptures. This requirement finds its source in the spiritual urge God has placed in us, so that a Christian

prays not because of divine law or human need, but as a loving response of a living soul.

2. *Because God gives* his grace and Holy Spirit to those only who continually ask them of him and are grateful for them. Now it is true: no one can ask for God's grace until God leads him to ask for that. And no one can ask for the Holy Spirit unless the Holy Spirit already in his soul interceded. Call that reasoning in a circle if you must, but it is a circle as boundless as the universe or God himself. We know that at the center is the love of the heavenly Father, upon whom we do not call in vain.

So logically prayer is still a mystery, neither defined by us nor explained in the Catechism. But theologically prayer is still a necessity both demanded by God and experienced by us. As a Christian — do you pray thankfully? Continually?

1. Why is prayer the chief part of gratitude?
2. Is prayer superfluous, superstitious or auto-suggestive?
3. Name some descriptions of prayer.
4. What forms of prayer are found in other religions?
5. Why does a Christian pray, if God is omniscient?
6. Is prayer a legal command or a spiritual necessity?
7. How does prosperity or adversity affect prayer?
8. What is the place of the Holy Spirit in prayer?

## Requisites of Prayer

QUESTION 117 — *What are the requisites of that prayer, which is acceptable to God, and which he will hear?*

ANSWER — First, that we from the heart pray to the one true God only, who hath manifested himself in his Word, for all things he hath commanded us to ask of him; secondly, that we rightly and thoroughly know our need and misery, that so we may deeply humble ourselves in the presence of his divine majesty; thirdly, that we be fully persuaded, that he, notwithstanding we are unworthy of it, will, for the sake of Christ our Lord, certainly hear our prayer, as he has promised us in his Word.

●

Without entering upon any discussion regarding liturgical or extemporaneous prayer, pastoral, personal or family prayer, silent, audible or prayers in unison, all prayers which God will hear must be acceptable to him. Acceptable prayer requires:

(1) *Our heart as the source and the true God as its aim.* A child learns to *say* its prayers, but when we *pray* our prayers our heart enters in, as well as our mind. The only true God is the

triune God who has revealed himself in his Word. Hence prayers to the saints — dead or alive — are excluded. There is only one God and only one kind of worship. Human philosophies and vague imagination regarding prayer to a "Supreme Being" are of no avail. We must call on the true God for all things he has commanded us to ask of him.

We must also raise our objection to Christians who pray to Jesus to the exclusion of God the Father or God the Spirit, as if Jesus were more familiar or more readily accessible. We may pray to Jesus, but Jesus is not the object but the basis of our prayer. Scriptural prayer is to God the Father, God the Son and God the Holy Spirit.

(2) *Knowledge of our need and misery.* Such a knowledge presupposes Biblical instruction regarding our real, our spiritual need, so that our prayers are on a higher level. Like a person subject to a fatal disease does not concern himself first of all in regard to matters of minor importance like amusement or clothes, so when through God's Word we learn of our real need we ask for forgiveness, a new heart, regeneration. And still more: we see our lack of spiritual graces and virtues which we only partially possess. In the mirror of God's Word we see how far short we are in view of our possibilities, so that we humble ourselves before God and our prayers will be more than a mere recital of needs common to all men, or a repetition of words committed to memory.

(3) *The Sacrifice of Christ* (Belgic Conf. Art. 26). We must be fully persuaded that in spite of our unworthiness our prayers are heard for Christ's sake. Jesus said: "I am the way, and the truth, and the life; no man cometh unto the Father but by me" (John 14:6). Many persons, therefore, would no more think of closing their prayer without saying "Amen," than they would forget to add: "In Jesus' name," or a similar expression. We approve of that, provided it is not a mere pious ending, or a superstitious sesame, but the expression of a persuasion that Christ is the way to God and that we accept his sacrifice for our sin as the basis for our petitions.

1. Name prayers for different occasions.
2. When is prayer acceptable to God?
3. Whence is the source of prayer?
4. To whom do we pray?
5. Do we pray to the three persons in the Trinity?
6. Why is knowledge of our personal need required?
7. Why do we pray in Jesus' name?
8. Quote examples in Scripture of answered prayers.

# Our Needs and Prayer

QUESTION 118 — *What hath God commanded us to ask of him?*

ANSWER — All things necessary for soul and body, which Christ our Lord has comprised in that prayer he himself has taught us.

●

Consider this word "commanded." That is literally true. We are taught that men ought to pray. We are told: Pray without ceasing. These are only a few samples of Biblical injunctions commanding us to pray. But we have already seen that prayer is beyond commandment and law and its bondage. Nevertheless many people act as if prayer were a mere commandment and not a spiritual communion. "It is time to pray," before meals. So we pray in church and in various meetings, because it is commanded. Do not forget: prayer is a Christian duty, but here the emphasis is upon prayer as a conscious, spiritual urge, which as a divine law within us we cannot help but obey.

Viewed in this light, the contents of that prayer appear rather limited: "for soul and body." Do we close the door to the needs of Church and State, the needy, the afflicted, the wandering, the doubting, the distress of millions on our globe? And then just "soul and body"? Yes, for soul and body (not just *my* soul and *my* body) send out sympathetic lines of communications to all these interests everywhere, and are related to all situations confronting souls and bodies. Their joy is our joy and their sorrow is our sorrow. Clear as glass the Lord's Prayer illumines these common needs so well as we begin: *Our Father.*

May we pray the Lord's Prayer? To our iconoclastic generation, this question may seem superfluous, yet in many of our Reformed churches its use was reduced to a minimum only a few decades ago. Partly this was due to a reaction against the Roman Catholic practice of vain repetition. But the opposition to its unrestrained use was born of a pietistic conviction that the unconverted could not say "Our Father," when he is not born into the divine family, and does not have the spirit of adoption, for Jesus taught this prayer to his disciples. However, in Matthew all the multitude was taught to pray, and not just the disciples. If this were a valid objection, then we could not pray to God in any Scriptural language, nor praise God in any spiritual song. Many — not to say most — spiritual expressions are often more ideal than real, but the higher ideal can inspire the lower attitude and lead to spiritual heights and depths when used by the Holy Spirit for our conviction and conversion.

How often should we pray the Lord's Prayer? In every family circle at least once a day. Every liturgical prayer in our Reformed Church liturgy culminated in the Lord's Prayer. The true liturgical use of the Lord's Prayer is again coming to its own in our churches at public worship. Not after the Invocation, but as an essential part of the pastoral prayer in which the congregation audibly participates.

May that prayer continue to be the expression of transcending personal needs, uniting us with all the saints into true communion with God in Christ!

1. Is prayer a duty or a spiritual need?
2. For what are we to pray?
3. What does "soul and body" refer to?
4. Why do we call this prayer the "Lord's" Prayer?
5. May all people pray the Lord's Prayer?
6. Is it enough to recite or repeat that prayer?
7. How often should we pray that prayer?
8. Where is the place in the Liturgy for it?

## The Lord's Prayer

QUESTION 119 — *What are the words of that prayer?*

ANSWER — Our Father which art in heaven, hallowed be thy name. Thy kingdom come. Thy will be done, on earth, as it is in heaven. Give us this day our daily bread, and forgive us our debts, as we forgive our debtors, and lead us not into temptation, but deliver us from evil, for thine is the kingdom, and the power, and the glory, forever. Amen.

This prayer is admirably described as "the purest expression of spiritual life as well as the most thorough test of spiritual life." Because of our familiarity we do not even approach to this deep appreciation. Like the benevolent rays of the sun are taken for granted and we hardly ever think of them in terms of life and light, so the Lord's Prayer suffers similarly. We have said it, sung it, prayed it, repeated it so often, that we give little attention or appreciation to its form or contents. Soon we intend to bathe our souls in the light of every facet of this precious diamond; just now a brief meditation on this prayer as a unit will give us a clearer insight and deeper appraisement, when we learn that this prayer is —

*Concise.* Here, indeed, is a prayer that infant lips can try.

Jesus taught his disciples, infants in the faith when they compared their inefficiency in prayer with the well-proportioned petitions of the Pharisees. These simple fishermen could pray this prayer! This brief prayer reveals the Master's touch. To write **the world's history in** ponderous volumes would be a gigantic task; to write this history in a few words would be an exquisite art. The Ten Commandments and the Beatitudes are similar instances of concise statements. Here we have it in prayer!

*Comprehensive* in its world-wide appeal. *Multum in parvo* is not always applicable to brief statements because they lack content. Not so in the Lord's Prayer. Here Jesus focused the higher glory that can be ascribed to the deity, and the deepest need that can be experienced by humanity in the brilliant light of this comprehensive prayer.

*Complete* in its trinitarian form. When we grasp its threefold arrangement, there is no objection concerning artificiality; in fact, its very presence is often overlooked. Yet here we find portrayed God the Father, infinitely great yet condescending his kindness in giving us our daily bread; God the Son who rules in his Kingdom and forgives us our debts; and God the Holy Spirit whose will is supreme and guides our will in temptation.

*Consistent* in its theological harmony: adoration, supplication and doxology. The adoration is threefold: Our, Father, Heaven. The supplication is twice threefold: three concerning God: Thy name, Thy kingdom, Thy will. And three for us: our bread, our debts and our temptations. The Doxology is threefold: the kingdom, the power, the glory.

For those who still regret that the name of Jesus is not in this prayer, let them be assured, that when we use Jesus' own words we pray in Jesus' name and the gates of heaven will be opened.

Viewed in this light, it may dawn on us that the Lord's Prayer for us too, is "the purest expression of spiritual life" in the consciousness of man's highest aim; and "the most thorough test of spiritual life" in the revelation of man's deepest need. Let us pray this prayer prayerfully.

1. How is the Lord's Prayer described?
2. Do we remove familiarity by neglecting it?
3. Why is this prayer concise?
4. How does it reach to divine heights?
5. To what human need does it respond?
6. Is the Trinity portrayed in this prayer?
7. Describe its threefold arrangement.
8. Do we pray in Jesus' name in this prayer?

# Our Father

QUESTION 120 — *Why hath Christ commanded us to address God thus, "Our Father"?*

ANSWER — That immediately in the very beginning of our prayer, he might excite in us a child-like reverence for, and confidence in God, which are the foundation of our prayer: namely, that God has become our Father in Christ, and will much less deny us what we ask of him in true faith, than our parents will refuse us earthly things.

QUESTION 121 — *Why is it here added, "which art in heaven"?*

ANSWER — Lest we should form any earthly conceptions of God's heavenly majesty, and that we may expect from his almighty power all things necessary for soul and body.

●

"Our Father who art in heaven" is an ascription and not a description of an authorized or official address. It is an address, but it is more: it is an invocation; it is the expression of the believer's attitude. Bearing this in mind, we do not here explore the theological basis of the Fatherhood of God, for that was explained in the study of the creed: I believe in God the Father. Only on that basis can we be the children of God.

Here the believer's acceptance of that Biblical explanation of the Fatherhood of God as the basis for his petition, explains the believer's attitude which he now assumes, and in which he confidently comes to the Supreme God of the universe in his childlike expression: *Our Father which art in heaven.*

Hence the explanation makes no apology nor minces words concerning any dogmatic controversy of those who have the right and others who just take the right to call God their Father. For this is a prayer, not a specific doctrine of theology. Christ has commanded us to address God thus, so that in the very beginning certain truths may come to our spiritual consciousness, certain assurances may be aroused in us, and certain comforts may be awakened in us. Thus we are taught to address God that Christ might "excite in us" acknowledgment of:

1. *Child-like reverence.* Reverence is akin to fear. Not in the sense of dread, but fear with the meaning of deep respect. (I Peter

2:17). And this God is not the Great Unknown, or a cruel tyrant, but our heavenly Father. And still he is so great, so majestic, so worthy of our worship that slip-shod familiarity is entirely out of place. Reverence is the first requisite in worship.

In the fellowship of the saints, it is a blessed experience to feel the importance of the plural statement *our*. However, unbiblical emphasis is dangerous practice. *Our* Father must be *my* Father first. Then we conceive of our common needs, which our Father will not deny us when we ask of him in true faith.

2. *Heavenly majesty.* We are not to form any earthly conceptions of God's heavenly majesty. *In heaven.* Unconsciously we look heavenward in our prayer. Our God is immanent, but he is also transcendent. How transcendent is God? The original has the distinct plural form *in the heavens,* and is distinguished from *heaven* in the third petition, the realm of the redeemed. Here the heavens of the 19th Psalm is meant; the heavens which declare the glory of God, and the clouds which Nahum calls the dust of his feet, and the universe beyond our conception of space limit. So transcendent is our God.

3. *Almighty power.* We may expect from his almighty power all things necessary for soul and body. Nothing is beyond his power, hence we may ask great things from God. There may be the limitation of our ability to use; there may be chastisement and unanswered prayer; there may be long delay: but all according to his will and all within his power.

Thus understood, these words "excite in us" the assurance that God's child does not call in vain when reverently he begins his prayer: *Our Father which art in heaven.*

1. Why do we address God as "Our Father"?
2. How does God become our Father?
3. May all people use these words?
4. What do these words arouse in us?
5. Does the word **our** add to the blessings of Christian fellowship?
6. Explain the words "in Heaven."
7. What do we expect from God's almighty power?
8. Have we assurance that prayer will be answered?

# God's Name

QUESTION 122 — *Which is the first petition?*

ANSWER — "Hallowed be thy name," that is, grant us first rightly to know thee, and to sanctify, glorify and praise thee in all thy works, in which thy power, wisdom, goodness, justice, mercy and truth, are clearly displayed; and further also, that we may so order and direct our whole lives, our thoughts, words and actions, that thy name may never be blasphemed, but rather honored and praised on our account.

●

We are not left in the dark concerning the true intent of the first, second, and third petition. Immediately this first objective petition is subjectively explained. It is not merely a pious wish or a sanctimonious exclamation, as if we said: let it be so, regardless of my part in it. At the very beginning the emphasis in the explanation is laid on our interest and activity. Thus we pray that God's name may be:

1. *Sanctified in us.* When we know God's name, we learn to know God's perfections. God revealed himself by various names when special circumstances required special assurances. So God revealed himself as Elohim, he that is to be feared. To Abraham: El-Shaddai, the Almighty, when Abraham could but marvel at God's promises. To Moses: Jehovah, I am. With every new name, the perfections of his being were revealed. Think of Jehovah-Jireh; Jehovah-Tsidkenu; Jehovah-Shalom; Jehovah-Nissi; Jehovah Shammai; Jehovah-Rophi; Jehovah-Ropheka. Should we add the more than 200 names given to our Lord Jesus Christ, we still would not reach the end, for God's name is identified with his Word: Acts 9:15; his service: Micah 4:5; his work: Psalm 8:1; his will: Job 1:21; his salvation: Acts 4:12. Then there are many titles which theologians do not classify as names, like Father, Judge, King, Rock, Shepherd, but which are valuable and instructive in their metaphorical descriptions.

2. *Sanctified through us.* "Grant that we may so order our lives, thoughts, words and actions that thy name may never be blasphemed, but rather be honored and praised on our account." No, we do not aim at adding holiness to God's name, for we cannot conceive of adding to perfection. Yet God's name is sanctified through us in a negative way when we heed the warning of the third commandment by not taking God's name in vain. Here the

word of warning is blasphemy, which means to revile or to abuse or to vilify. And that covers the territory of our "whole lives, our thoughts, words and actions." How offensive to God must much of our behavior appear! How utterly degrading for one who knows these wonderful, meaningful names to drag them through the dirt of disrespect!

Positively, God's name is sanctified through us when that name is "honored and praised on our account." Let us never think of that as something we must do, but rather consider it a privilege that we may do it, and as a marvel of God's grace that we can do it.

Let no one say or pray thoughtlessly: ". . . hallowed be thy name." It could mean more than we thought. Let us pray it sincerely and effectively, lest when we hold our peace, "the stones would immediately cry out." "Take the name of Jesus with you" in your worship, your witness, and your work.

1. Where is the first emphasis in the Lord's Prayer?
2. How is God's name sanctified in us?
3. Why is God's name of such importance?
4. How many names of God the Father do you know?
5. How many names of God the Son do you know?
6. How many names of God the Spirit do you know?
7. How is that name sanctified in us, negatively?
8. How is that name sanctified in us, positively?

# God's Kingdom

QUESTION 123 — *Which is the second petition?*

ANSWER — "Thy Kingdom come," that is, rule us so by thy Word and Spirit, that we may submit ourselves more and more to thee; preserve and increase thy Church, destroy the works of the devil, and all violence which would exalt itself against thee; and also, all wicked counsels devised against thy holy Word; till the full perfection of thy kingdom takes place, wherein thou shalt be all in all.

●

David, the king, ascribed unto the Lord the real honor in his prayer, I Chron. 29:11: "Thine is the kingdom, O Lord," and great David's greater Son, our Lord Jesus Christ, teaches us to pray: "Thy kingdom come." Again and again did Jesus use the phrase "kingdom of heaven" in parable and preaching, and never did we have difficulty or hesitation in understanding the significance of this expression to mean the complete message of salvation.

Only in recent years the unbiblical distinction between the kingdom and the Church became the battleground among believers. However, the Catechism still adheres to the old interpretation and at the very outset explains this phrase: Preserve and increase thy *Church*.

Jesus is King. The Psalmist sang: "His kingdom ruleth over all." The prophets foretold it (Isaiah 9:7), the angel announced it (Luke 1:33), and Jesus' first message was: "Repent, for the kingdom of heaven is at hand." Amidst the silence of his suffering he replied to Pilate's question: "Art thou a king, then?" "Thou sayest it."

With all this in mind, when we pray this petition, we are taught that this kingdom of Jesus is to be:

1. *Established* in every human soul by his Word and Spirit. Without the regenerating power of these two agencies we cannot even see the kingdom of God. That kingdom is established in every regenerated soul and in every Christian home and in every Christian Church where Jesus is, Acts 2:36, "both Lord and Christ."

2. *Preserved and increased.* Building the kingdom is building the Church. The growth and the spread of the kingdom is the hope and the joy of the Church. Yes, the Church must be preserved and increased and prayer is an effective means to that end: "Pray ye the Lord of the harvest." Here the believer is mission-minded and through this prayer is stirred into whole-souled mission-zeal.

3. *Defended.* "Destroy the works of the devil," for there is a kingdom of darkness which displays "violence which would exalt itself against thee." How many souls have become victims of this evil power! The natural man is still the tool of the devil, resulting in persecutions and martyrdom from Cain to Calvary to Communism. The carnal Christian in his lukewarmness and indifference is a stumblingblock to the progress of the kingdom in missions.

4. *Victorious.* "Till the full perfection of thy kingdom takes place." We do not pray in doubt or in vain. We know that the day shall come when the kingdoms of the world shall become the kingdom of Christ.

In so far as we are ruled by God's Word and Spirit, helping to preserve and to increase the Church and being active in destroying the works of the devil, do we rightly pray: "Thy kingdom come."

1. Mention instances of Jesus' use of "Kingdom" in parable, preaching, prayer.
2. What do we mean by "Kingdom"?
3. Is this word applied to the Church?
4. Where is Jesus King now?
5. How is the Church preserved, increased?
6. How must the works of the devil be destroyed?
7. What will be the final outcome?
8. Does this encourage us in missionary efforts?

# God's Will

QUESTION 124 — *Which is the third petition?*

ANSWER — "Thy will be done on earth as it is in heaven," that is, grant that we and all men may renounce our own will, and without murmuring obey thy will, which is only good; that so every one may attend to, and perform the duties of his station and calling, as willingly and faithfully as the angels do in heaven.

●

This is the third petition that has both an objective aim and a subjective application. To merely admit the first and to neglect the second is to misunderstand and to misapply the teaching of Jesus. We ask:

1. *What is God's will?* It is the constitution of the kingdom of God. Much of that will is secret. In God's providence, predestination and prophecy we recognize the will of God concerning which we learn to say: Thy will be done, in the sense of being submissive to it. When in God's providence sickness comes and we pray for recovery which does not materialize, a Christian finds comfort when he learns to say: Have thine own way, Lord. But that will of God is not meant here. To interpret it as such is an evidence of mystical piety indicating unhealthy spiritual life. Here we meet with God's revealed will. Whereas God's secret will requires submission, God's revealed will demands obedience. God's revealed will is in the Bible: "This is the will of God, even your sanctification." Obedience to God's will requires faith, conviction and consecration.

**2. *Where is God's will obeyed?*** In heaven, the place of God's perfect, undisputed sovereignty, where his angels perform his will willingly and faithfully in their station and calling. Grasping beyond that, to touch God in his sovereign will, was the sin of the fallen angels who were cast out. Heaven is a state of perfection where God's angels do his commandments, hearkening unto the voice of his word (Ps. 103:20). On earth, too, these angels perform God's will: they announced our Saviour's birth and one appeared unto him from heaven strengthening him in Gethsemane. One delivered Peter from prison and one stood by Paul on the sinking ship. Nor are we deprived from their benevolent service. "Are they not all ministering spirits, sent forth to minister for them who shall be heirs of salvation" (Heb. 1:14)?

**3. *How must God's will still be obeyed?*** Having the angels in heaven as our example and inspiration, we pray to be enabled to do likewise on earth. To accomplish this we need (a) sincere prayer to renounce our own will, for our wills are evil. In the school of Christ we learn to pray: Lord, what wilt thou have me do? We do not graduate from that school immediately. (b) Joyful obedience: without murmuring, for obedience while murmuring drains the blessing from the deed. (c) Spiritual contentment with our "station and calling." True, that includes the office of our leaders in Church, school and State, and often we criticize them severely. But it also includes the workman on the bench; the mother in the kitchen; the child in the home; the man behind the plough and the cleaner of the street. There are no menial tasks when we recognize God's hand in our "station and calling."

Rightly prayed, this petition would surround the hum-drum of life with a glorified radiancy. It could transform this earth to a little bit of heaven.

1. Is this petition merely objective?
2. What is God's will?
3. What is God's secret will?
4. What does God's revealed will require of us?
5. Where do angels carry out God's will?
6. How is that an example for us?
7. Name three requirements for such obedience.
8. Discuss our station and calling in relation to the will of God.

# Our Bread

QUESTION 125 — *Which is the fourth petition?*

ANSWER — "Give us this day our daily bread," that is, be pleased to provide us with all things necessary for the body, that we may thereby acknowledge thee to be the only fountain of all good, and that neither our care nor our industry, nor even thy gifts, can profit us without thy blessing, and therefore that we may withdraw our trust from all creatures, and place it alone in thee.

●

The Lord's Prayer is a God-centered prayer: there are three petitions in regard to God's sovereignty, and then there are three in regard to God's supply for us. Should someone criticize this petition for bread as being too materialistic for finding first place for God's supply in our need, we may point to the fact that God created us with a material body and maintains us with material means. We are not ashamed to share the Psalmist's conviction: "Thou openest thy hand, and satisfied the desire of every living thing" (Ps. 145:16). Moreover, as soon as we focus our attention on the words "us" and "our," that matter assumes a moral significance; and when we say "give" to God, there is a spiritual emphasis. Rather would we see Jesus' wisdom in presenting these three human needs in the scope of our complete cycle: the present — our daily bread; the past — our debts; the future — our victory over evil. Here we learn that this petition is:

1. *Comprehensive.* "Be pleased to provide us with all things necessary for the body." Bread? Yes, but what is bread without health? There is a wider application in all our physical needs, for our bread may mean the work of our hand or the skill of our mind, or the swiftness of our feet, or the strength of our back. Our annual Day of Prayer for Crops and Industry is a much-needed reminder. We pray for our *daily* bread. That means neither poverty nor riches nor anxiety about the future. Manna fell from heaven in daily supply. And *our* daily bread, points to that which is ours through honest labor, excluding laziness, theft or greed, but still it is not *mine* alone. When we say *our* we think of the needy neighbor, our fellowmen, whom we can supply with our abundance.

2. *Appropriate.* "That we may thereby acknowledge thee to

be the fountain of all good." Nothing, not even God's gifts, can profit us without his blessing. God's sovereignty and man's dependence are so appropriately stated when we pray *give* — even when we recall our heavy tasks and the never-ending toil in reaping the harvest. Even though our barns are filled, still we depend on God to *give,* withdrawing our trust from all creatures and placing it in God alone. And how true that is in the physical world. Somewhere on this earth the harvest is always being reaped, but mankind is never more than three months from starvation.

*3. Practical.* This petition truly prayed adds immeasurably to our spiritual stature. It makes us humble and content, for God supplies "each according to his ability." It makes us active for we may work for God when God works for us and with us. It makes us confident when we sow in tears that we shall reap in joy. It teaches us responsibility and generosity, for how can we be indifferent when a hungry child is knocking at our door? It gives us faith for the future in days that are dark, and in times of adversity we know he will provide.

1. What do we confess in this petition?
2. What is the emphasis of "us" and "our"?
3. What is the wider interpretation of "bread"?
4. What does "daily" teach us?
5. What do we acknowledge when we say "give"?
6. Why is the provision of food different from the supply of air and water?
7. What is the spiritual lesson in this petition?
8. What is the practical lesson in this petition?

## Our Debts

QUESTION 126 — *Which is the fifth petition?*

ANSWER — "And forgive us our debts, as we forgive our debtors," that is, be pleased, for the sake of Christ's blood, not to impute to us, poor sinners, our transgressions, nor that depravity which always cleaves to us; even as we feel this evidence of thy grace in us, that it is our firm resolution, from the heart to forgive our neighbor.

What a wide variety of interpretations has been given to this petition! In the time of Chrysostom, the ancient Church father, Christians did not dare to pray this, in order not to bring the curse upon them in their unforgiving attitude to others. Perfectionists hold that they do not need to pray this for they no longer find sin in themselves. We often pray it thoughtlessly, but we ought to pray it with a firm grasp of faith in regard to its real meaning. This petition contains for the believer:

1. *A Revelation.* The possibility and the reality of the forgiveness of sin. This is the great message of the revealed Word of God. Human hearts do not practice it, and human courts do not proclaim it. Voices of remorse, like ghosts of the past, disturb our peace. Time may silence our accusing conscience, like nature hides her ravages after the storm while the scars remain. Christianity alone knows of a God with whom there is forgiveness, and a Lamb of God that taketh away the sin of the world. To be sure, we were founded on that faith in Question 56, as part of the Apostles' Creed, but this is no mere repetition. There it was a part of our Confession, here it is a prayer. There it was to escape condemnation; here it is to grow in sanctification. There it was one of the three gifts to the Church; here it is a Christian's personal privilege and practice. That, too, is the answer to the question whether regenerated Christians should still pray this: there is such a thing as a daily conversion and a daily turning to the Lord for forgiveness. Did we love God with all our heart, mind and strength? Did we love our neighbor as ourselves? Are there not many sins of omission? There is a "depravity which always cleaves to us."

2. *A Remedy.* "Be pleased for the sake of Christ's blood not to impute to us our transgressions." With our sins, our shortcomings, our frailties, our imperfections, we must go again and again to the fountain, Christ. The Church does not forgive. Our religious activities do not atone. The minister cannot do it. The priest may say "absolvo te," but only God, against whom we have transgressed, can forgive. Nor does an appeal to the Old Testament procedure clear the unbiblical practice of the Confessional of the Roman Catholic Church. The Old Testament priest pronounced the leper clean after God had made him clean, but the priest did not make him clean. Nor can a priest do this now. He can pronounce him clean from sin, when God for Christ's sake has forgiven him.

3. *A Reminder.* "As we forgive our debtors." Not in the perfect measure of equality as we need forgiveness, for then there is little hope for us. In Luke we read *for,* but even this *for* is not causal but indicative. Consider the unjust steward in

Luke 16. That willingness to forgive is rightly stated as "an evidence of thy grace in us." With that in mind, how often must we forgive others? As often as we need to ask forgiveness of God!

1. Why did some early Christians not pray this petition?
2. Do perfectionists pray this prayer?
3. How ought we to pray it?
4. Is the use of "trespasses" permissible?
5. How does this petition differ from our Confession about forgiveness?
6. Should the regenerated pray this petition too?
7. For whose sake are our transgressions not imputed unto us?
8. What is the "evidence of grace" in us as related to the second part of this petition?

## Our Temptations

QUESTION 127 — *Which is the sixth petition?*

ANSWER — "And lead us not into temptation, but deliver us from evil;" that is, since we are so weak in ourselves, that we cannot stand a moment; and besides this, since our mortal enemies, the devil, the world, and our own flesh cease not to assault us; do thou, therefore, preserve and strengthen us by the power of thy Holy Spirit, that we may not be overcome in this spiritual warfare, but constantly and strenuously may resist our foes, till at last we obtain a complete victory.

●

Embedded in subjective interpretation, this petition forms a breeding ground for doubt and criticism, as if God induces man to evil. For the Christian, two facts stand like stone: God cannot be tempted with evil, neither tempteth he any man (Jas. 1:4). Yet these expressions are used in the Bible. To tempt in the sense of to induce has an evil implication, while to tempt in the sense of to test has no such meaning.

For a realistic, Scriptural interpretation of this petition we ask:

1. *What is its significance?* Temptations, then, come to us for our (a) *testing.* Abraham was so tested in his faith. "The Lord thy God proveth thee, to know whether ye love the Lord" (Deut. 13:3). Temptations come to us for our (b) *discipline.* By God's permissive will, Job was tested to prove his loyalty to God

and he did not fail but came to good conclusions. They come to us for building up our (c) *resistance*. Our first parents were tempted by the serpent and tested by God, who placed the tree of knowledge of good and evil in the garden. Such temptations build up a resistance against sin, like a tree grows strong roots when lashed by the storm. Character is not built in a sheltered spot. A mighty oak does not grow in a greenhouse.

2. *What is its purpose?* Why pray to escape this, when such results can be derived? It is true, James speaks about the blessing of enduring temptation, and David in Ps. 139 prayed, "Try me and search my heart." We *do* pray this, for testing is never a pleasant experience, and we are not stoics in our faith. We know our weaknesses, even though God tempers the wind for his shorn lamb. We may pray this, for God delivers by his Word and Spirit. We may pray this, so that being conscious of our weak spots, through prayer we invoke God's help and we learn to stand on our guard.

3. *What is its realization?* Complete victory is its aim, and to attain that we pray that "we may not be overcome in this spiritual warfare" and that we may be "preserved and strengthened by the power of thy Spirit." We admit that in our strength we cannot stand a moment against our mortal enemies: the devil, the world and our own flesh. But we do not stand alone. In this mighty struggle against the forces of evil within and without we have our High Priest who can have sympathy with us and was tempted in all things like we are, sin excepted. Facing our foes we learn to fight the good fight of faith until "at last" — until our dying day — we will be more than conquerors through him who has loved us, and obtain a complete victory.

1. Explain different meanings of "to tempt."
2. State Biblical instances of God's testing.
3. What is testing in the form of discipline?
4. Does testing build resistance?
5. How is character built?
6. Then why do we pray to escape temptation?
7. Who helps us in our temptations?
8. What must be the final outcome?

# The Doxology

QUESTION 128 — *How dost thou conclude thy prayer?*

ANSWER — "For thine is the kingdom, and the power, and the glory, forever," that is, all these we ask of thee, because thou, being our King and almighty, art willing and able to give us all good; and all this we pray for, that thereby, not we but thy holy name may be glorified forever.

⬤

What a glorious doxology for this God-centered prayer! Here, too, as at the beginning, this prayer lifts us again to God. So it should be, for prayer is communion, a lifting of the soul to God. What a loss for Roman Catholics who quote from Luke, where this doxology is omitted, but Matthew 6:13 records it. "Amen" is not recorded in Luke either, but there they quote from Matthew and use that. Very likely Jesus repeated this prayer several times, before the Evangelists could quote it as uniformly as they did. Besides, I Chron. 29:11 indicates a similar conclusion in Jewish prayers.

This doxology, beginning with the word *for,* points to the divine motive as the basis of our prayer. Not: Lord, save me, *for* I perish. Surely not: *for* I merit it. Here it indicates our acknowledgment of God as our King who in his almighty power is willing and able to fill our needs; and it indicates a willingness to submit the outcome of our prayer, whether it is unanswered or postponed, to the well-being of God's kingdom and the glory of God's name.

In this spirit we ascribe unto God: *Thine is the Kingdom.* Since our God is an almighty, eternal King, we do not aim to tell him how to rule, nor ask him to change his plan. Our prayers are subordinate to the will of the King. *And the power.* We pray because we believe God has the wisdom to rule and the power to establish that rule. When we say, thine is the power, we know that unanswered prayers are not such because God lacks power, but because his wisdom has better plans for us. Nor do we ascribe this attribute of power to God because we believe that there is another power equal to God's power. All power is of God. Satan has only permissive power, and that shall be taken from him. God has creating and maintaining power in the universe which are plainly seen in the starry skies and the changing seasons. And beyond all that is power of God unto salvation as revealed in the Gospel of Christ. With that power God did not send his Son to condemn the world, but that the world through him might be saved (John 3:17).

*And the glory, forever.* Praying this we promise that we will not credit ourselves nor give glory to the skill of others, when our prayers are heard. And even when our petitions are withheld all of life's experiences and vicissitudes are seen in the light of the glory of God. And that forever. The brief span of life is absorbed into eternity; our temporal needs are in charge of the everlasting God. Thus when the eye of faith has seen the glory of the Lord, Paul and Silas can sing songs in the night; the martyr dies bravely at the stake; and the humble believer faces dark providences with a joy that "lights up the clouds before life's sun goes down." He, too, "beheld his glory" (John 1:14).

1. Who do not use this doxology?
2. Is there O. T. authority for its use?
3. What does "for" mean in this petition?
4. What do we ascribe to God in this petition?
5. Differentiate God's power and Satan's power.
6. What is God's power unto salvation?
7. What do we promise in this doxology?
8. If our prayers are unanswered is this doxology still true?

# Amen

QUESTION 129 — *What doth the word "Amen" signify?*

ANSWER — *"Amen"* signifies, it shall truly and certainly be; for my prayer is more assuredly heard of God, than I feel in my heart that I desire these things of him.

●

A simple and most satisfactory explanation of this significant conclusion of our prayer was expressed by a child to be "that you mean it." And that definition could furnish sufficient material for a profitable application!

However, when we consider its propriety, a few additional remarks are in place. Even though not found in Luke, it is mentioned by Matthew, and the Jews had a similar custom, so that after the reading of the law Deut. *27* contains this statement twelve times: "And all the people shall say, Amen." Doing this, they expressed more than assent or approval but promised willing obedience.

The original meaning of this word is "to uphold," like a pillar or a foundation, so that we give a moral and spiritual support to what we have prayed by ending with "Amen," indicating that it shall truly and certainly be. For stronger than my sincere feeling of need, deeper than my earnest desire of my heart, is my faith that God hears my prayer.

Search the Scriptures, and you will be amazed and inspired by the various applications in the Bible of this word now understood in every language of Christendom. There is the meaning of *certainty*: II Cor. 1:20: "All the promises of God are in him yea, and in him Amen." Sometimes it indicates *assurance*: Ps. 106:8: "Let all the people say, Amen." In Rev. 1:7: *confirmation*: "Even so, Amen." In Rev. 3:14: Christ, the *truth*: "These things saith the Amen." Jesus used it by way of *affirmation* in his many expressions beginning with "verily, verily." *Agreement* is indicated in Ps. 72:19 and Ps. 41:13.

Then the question still remains: Who must say Amen? The one who prays, or the one to whom we pray? Is it proper in our prayer to say that to God? If we pray thoughtlessly, it is just a mere ending, or at the most a sanctimonious or magical conclusion. If God's revelation is our foundation and we pray in the Spirit, we may conclude with Amen, for then it contains the comforting assurance that our prayer is heard of God.

When are we to use this word, besides its use in prayer? Many use it during the sermon (I Cor. 14:16) but our Reformed fathers insisted on its use at the close of every sermon, and this practice should be restored where it is omitted. In formal worship services it is used after the singing of every hymn. Our Confession of Faith has this ending but many do not seem to know that. A threefold Amen sung by the choir can add reverence to the occasion, while a sevenfold Amen often seems like over-extending its usefulness. When the *pastor* prays with the sick it is a wholesome experience for the sick person reverently and audibly so to conclude with the pastor's prayer. We say it meekly and submissively in our trials, and we say it expectantly and triumphantly in our glorious hope: "Amen, even so come, Lord Jesus." And concluding the complete scope of doctrinal instruction of the Catechism, we, too, say it believingly: *Amen*.

1. Does the Gospel of Luke mention this?
2. Where is it found in Matthew?
3. Was "Amen" used in O.T. times?
4. What is its original meaning?
5. In what different applications is it used?
6. Mention expressions of Jesus, beginning with "Verily, verily."
7. May we, or must the minister, say Amen at the close?
8. Mention various religious occasions when "Amen" may be used.